FOOTBALL
RULES
ILLUSTRATED

FOOTBALL RULES ILLUSTRATED

Edited by George Sullivan

Produced by Charles Fellows

A FIRESIDE BOOK
Published by Simon & Schuster
New York London Toronto Sydney Tokyo Singapore

Rockefeller Center
1230 Avenue of the Americas
New York, New York 10020

FIRESIDE and colophon are registered
trademarks of Simon & Schuster, Inc.

Manufactured in the
United States of America

16

Library of Congress Cataloging in Publication Data

Sullivan, George, 1927-
  Football rules illustrated.

  1. Football—Rules. I. Title.
GV955.S93   796.332′02′022   81-12443
AACR2

ISBN: 0-671-61295-6

CONTENTS

INTRODUCTION

The few hundred spectators who showed up sat on the ground, on a rail fence, or in buckboards or carriages. Admission was free.

There were no uniforms. Despite a chill wind, the 25 players on each team simply shed their hats, coats, and vests.

The playing field was much larger than now, 360-feet long and 225 feet wide.

There were few rules. A goal, which had to be kicked, counted one point. Running with the ball or throwing it was not permitted, nor were tripping or holding. Otherwise, just about everything was tolerated.

In strict terms, it wasn't football at all, but a form of soccer.

Nevertheless, when Rutgers defeated Princeton, 6 goals to 4, on November 6, 1869, on Rutgers College Field, it marked the formal beginnings of American football.

The rules of the game have gone through enormous change since that time. In the 1880s, Walter Camp, who came to be known as the "Father of American Football," introduced the concept of the line of scrimmage, led the fight for eleven men on a side, and got the rulemakers to adopt a system of downs.

Through the years, the method of scoring the game has changed eight times, the size of the ball eight times, and the size of the field sixteen times.

These changes have opened up play, made it faster. And although they have also made the game somewhat more complex, it's still an easy game to follow.

In its original form, football would undoubtedly have survived, but just barely. There would have been no such national heroes as Tony Dorsett or Earl Campbell. There would have been no spectators by the millions, no huge stadiums.

There would have been no television. There would have been no time-outs for television commercials either. Few people complain, however. It's still better than watching from a buckboard or carriage.

Football Rules

OBJECT OF THE GAME

Two teams of 11 players each attempt to score points by kicking goals or putting the ball across the opponents' goal line. The winning team is the one that scores the greatest number of points.

THE FIELD

The rectangular playing field is 120 yards long and 53 1/3 yards wide. It is divided by parallel yard lines, 5 yards apart. These are intersected by short in-bounds lines 70 feet, 9 inches from each side line. Each of the lines used in try-for-point plays is within the playing field and 2 yards from its related goal line.

The lines at the ends of the field are called end lines. Those on each side of the field are called side lines. The goal lines are the lines 10 yards from and parallel to the end lines. The end zones are the areas bounded by the end lines, goal lines, and side lines.

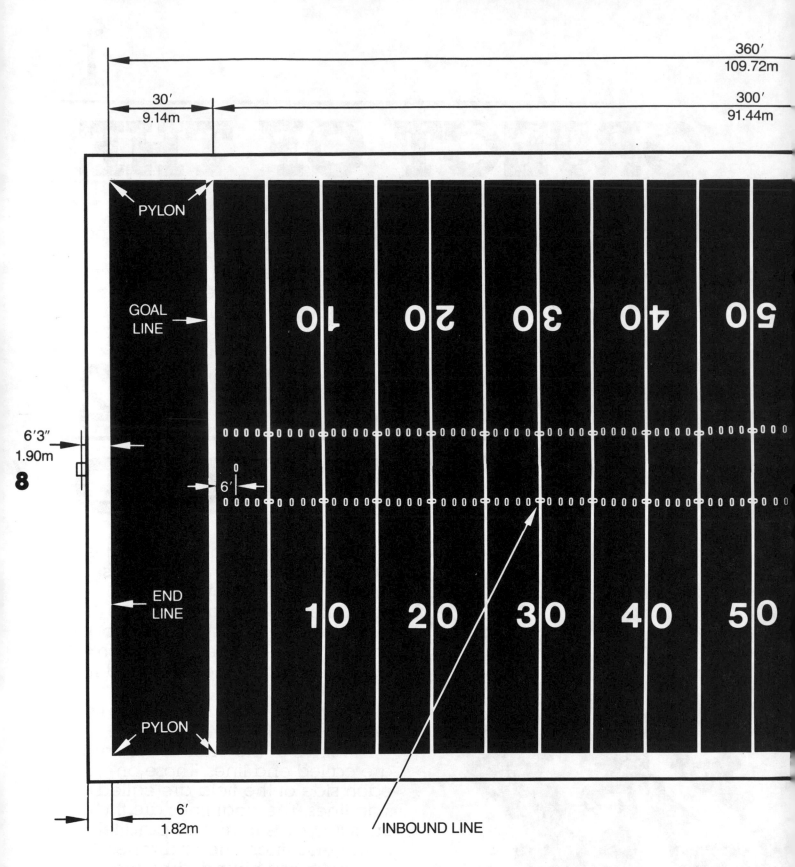

8

All measurements are made from the inside edges of the lines. The side lines and the end lines themselves are out-of-bounds. The goal lines are considered within the end zones.

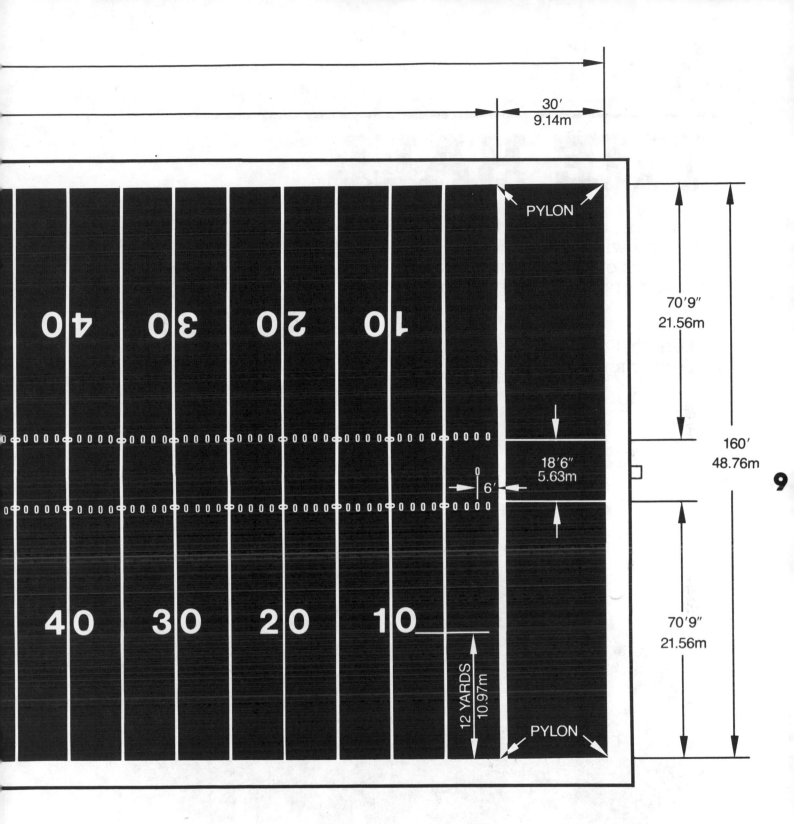

FOOTBALL FIELD DIAGRAM

3

THE BALL

The ball, an inflated bladder covered with pebbled grain leather, is oval with somewhat pointed ends. It has these dimensions:

Length: 11-11 1/2 inches
Short circumference: 21 1/4-21 1/2 inches
Long circumference: 28-28 1/2 inches
Weight: 14-15 ounces

GOAL POSTS

Goal posts are to be erected within the plane of each goal line. Each consists of a horizontal crossbar 18 feet, 6 inches in length. Its top surface is to be 10 feet

above the ground. At each end of the horizontal crossbar, there is a vertical upright. Each is 4 inches in diameter and extends at least 20 feet above the crossbar.

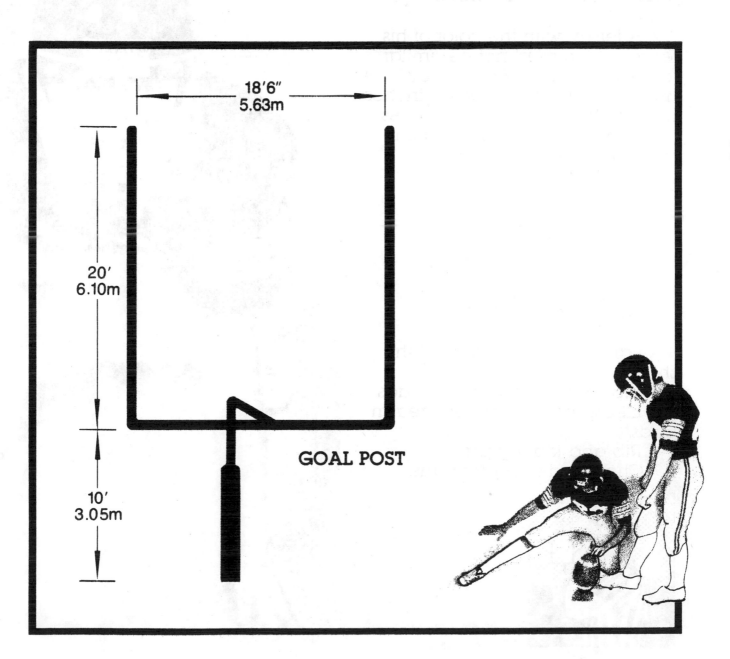

GOAL POST

5
EQUIPMENT

Each player wears:

1. A helmet made of plastic that is equipped with a face mask made of nonbreakable molded plastic, coated with rubber.

2. A jersey with the color of his team, which must not be similar to the color of the ball. Jersey numbers must be at least 8 inches high on the chest and 10 inches high on the back. Players are to be numbered as follows:

ends: 80-89
tackles: 70-79
guards: 60-69
centers: 50-59
fullbacks: 30-39
halfbacks: 20-29; 40-49
quarterbacks: 1-19

3. Pants, stockings, lightweight shoes.
4. Hip, thigh, knee, or shin pads.
5. Elbow, hand, wrist, or forearm pads.
6. Rib and kidney pads.
7. Chest and shoulder pads.

Football Rules

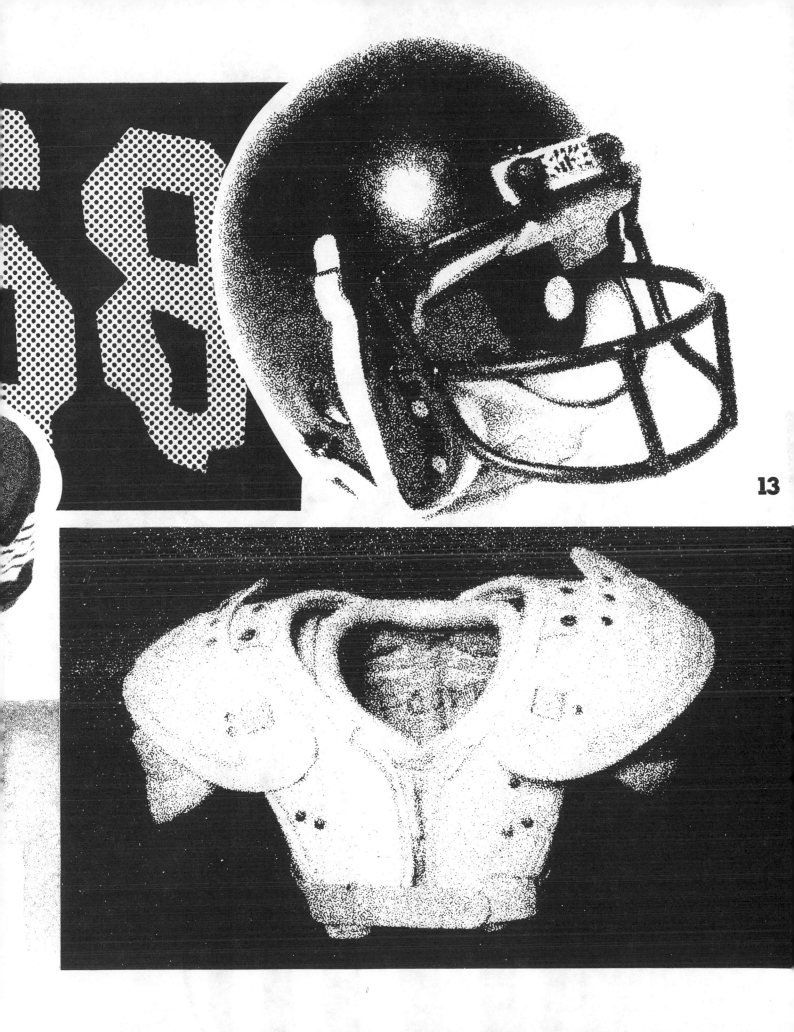

13

OFFICIALS

The officials and their duties are as follows:

1. Referee—Is in command of the seven-man crew. He lines up behind the offensive backfield and follows the ball. He starts and ends the game and signals when to stop and start the official clock. He notifies the coaches of time-outs and two-minute warnings. Announces options on penalties, unless automatic.

2. Umpire—Lines up in the middle of the defensive backfield. Checks interior linemen for illegal holding and supervises the short-pass area. Notes linemen downfield on passes. Keeps track of time-outs.

3. Head Linesman—Checks offside. Supervises the chain crew, checking that the rods are set properly. Marks out-of-bounds on his side of the field. Watches for illegal receivers.

4. Field Judge—Covers kicks from scrimmage, passes crossing the defensive goal line, and loose balls. Looks for illegal substitutions. Times intermission between halves. Signals when ball is dead or time-out has been called. Responsible for continuing action fouls and decisions involving catching, recovery, out-of-bounds spot, illegal touching, and loose ball across the line of scrimmage. Checks kicker and height and tee. Notifies teams five minutes before start of the second half. Watches for pass interference.

5. Back Judge—Lines up on the same side of the field as the line judge. Checks number of defensive players. Checks when ball is dead and when time is out. Assists in decisions involving catching, recovery, or illegally touching a loose ball beyond the line of scrimmage. Rules on plays involving the pass receiver, including the legality of the catch or pass interference.
Calls clipping penalties on punt returns. Assists field judge in deciding whether field-goal attempts are successful.

6. Line Judge—Responsible for timing the game. Records all time-outs. Watches for illegal motion behind the line of scrimmage or illegal shifts. Fires pistol to signal end of each period. Notifies referee when two minutes remain in each half. Assists the referee in detecting holding violations, false

1 REFEREE
2 UMPIRE
3 LINESMAN
4 FIELD JUDGE
5 BACK JUDGE
6 LINE JUDGE

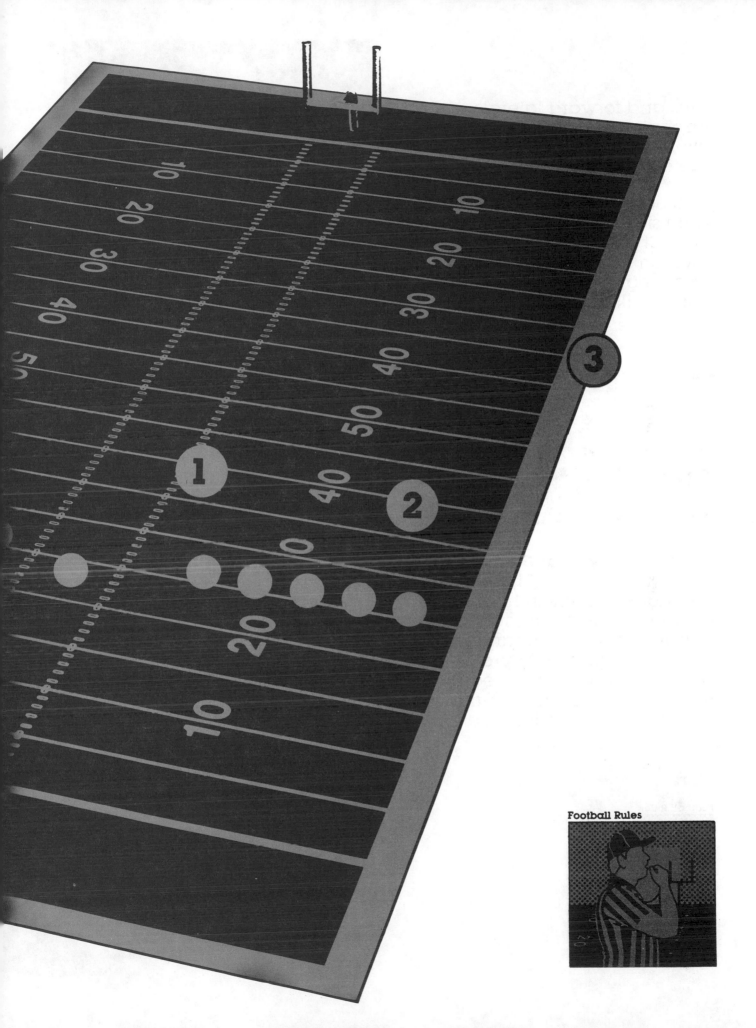

Football Rules

starts and forward laterals. Assists umpire in detecting holding violations. Marks out-of-bounds on his side of the field.

7. Side Judge—Lines up on the same side of field as head linesman. Checks wide receiver and back on that side of the field, observing their blocks and actions taken against them.

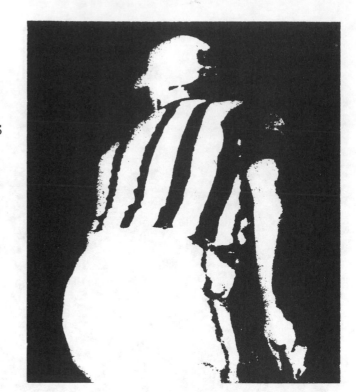

7

TIMING

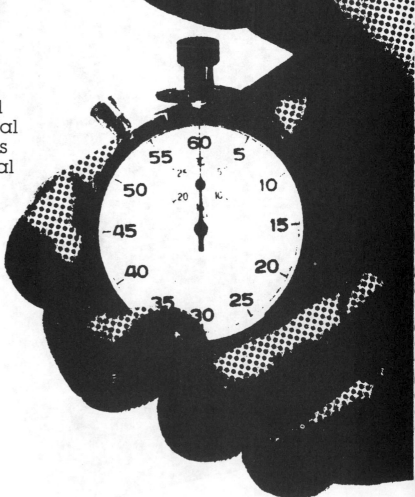

The game is played in four 15-minute quarters. (There are 12-minute quarters in high-school play.) There is a 15-minute interval at halftime. Teams change goals after each quarter. In professional play, ties may be decided by means of one or more 15-minute sudden-death overtime periods.

Football Rules

PLAYERS

Each team fields 11 players, one of whom is the captain. There must be seven offensive players on the line of scrimmage when the ball is snapped. They are the center, two guards, two tackles, and two ends (receivers). In the backfield, at least one yard behind the line, are four backs—a quarterback, a fullback, and two halfbacks. Any player may run with the ball, but only the two ends and backs are eligible to catch a forward pass.

There are no restrictions in the way the defensive linemen can line up. Normally, there are either four or five linemen—two tackles, two ends, and sometimes a middle guard—on the line of scrimmage. Behind the line, there are two or three linebackers and four defensive backs—two corner-backs and two safeties.

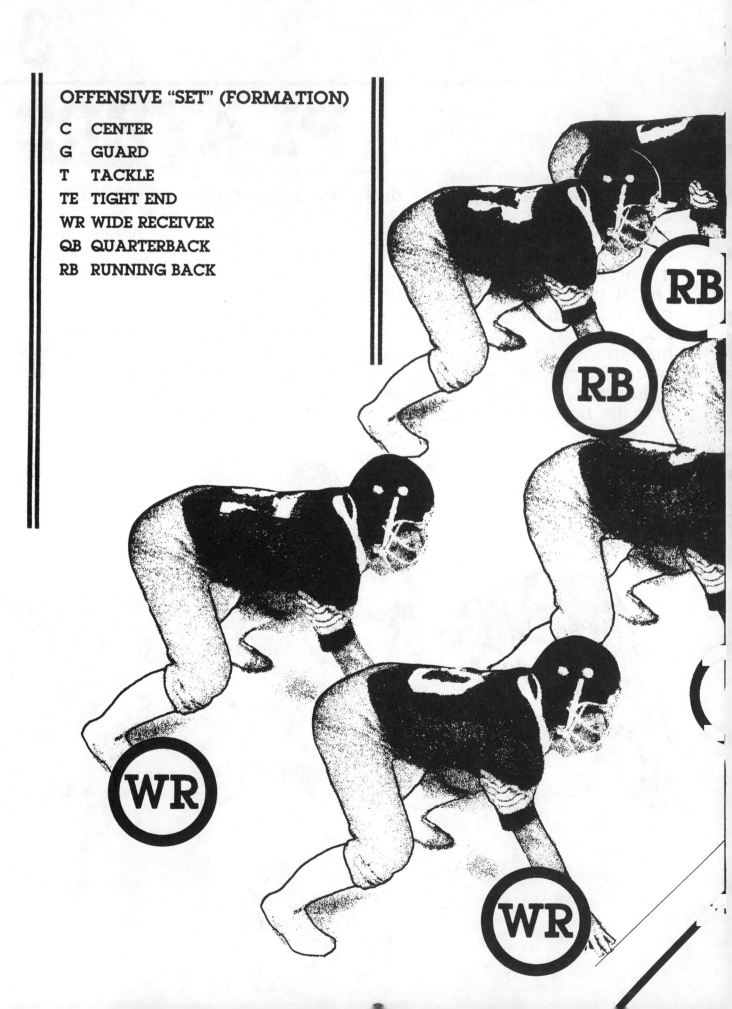

OFFENSIVE "SET" (FORMATION)

C   CENTER
G   GUARD
T   TACKLE
TE TIGHT END
WR WIDE RECEIVER
QB QUARTERBACK
RB RUNNING BACK

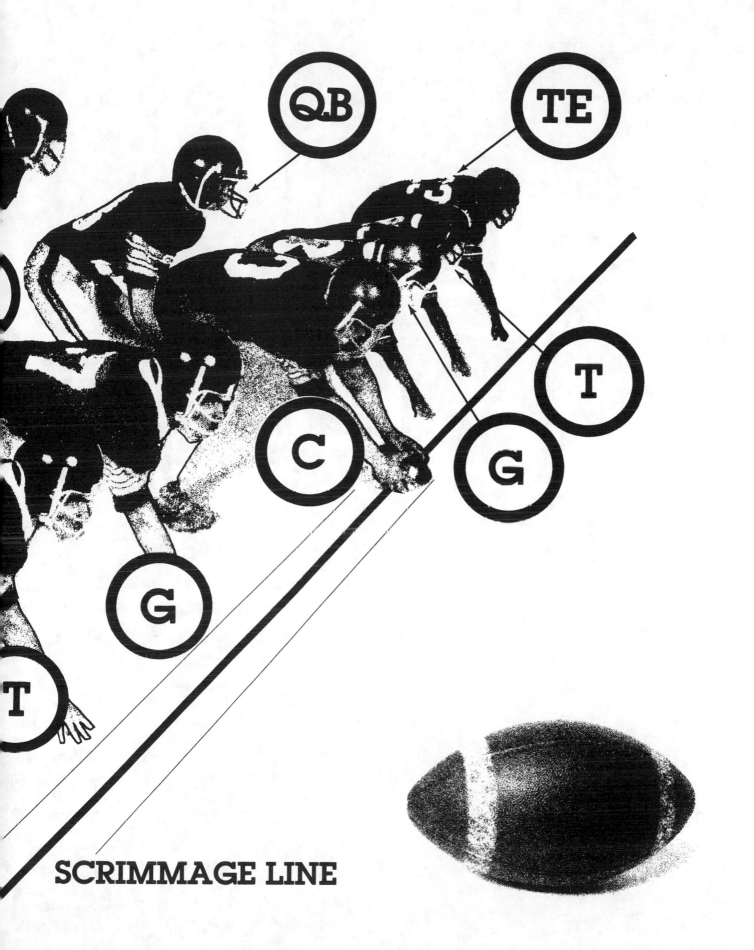

QB

TE

T

G

C

G

T

SCRIMMAGE LINE

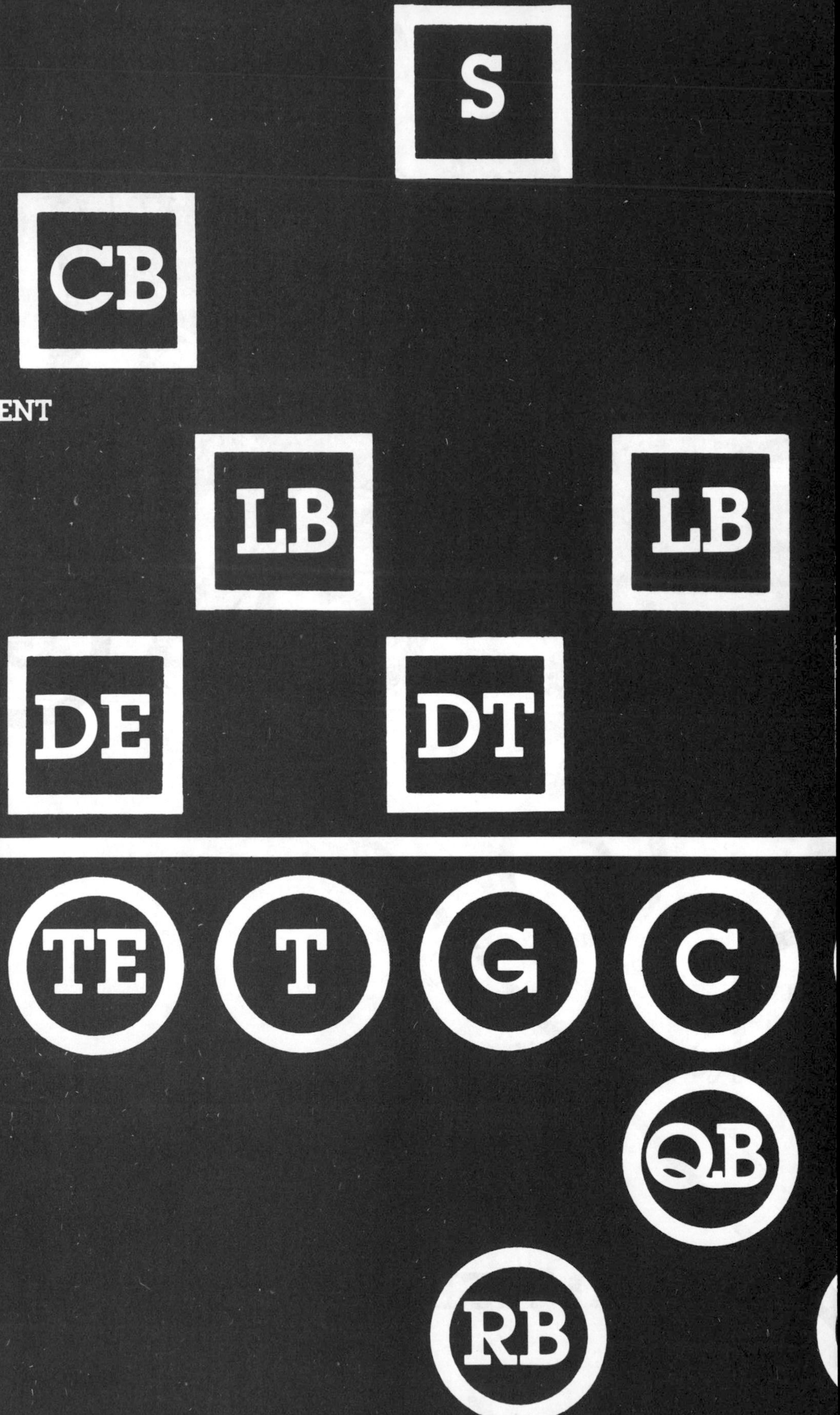

S

CB

DEFENSIVE ALIGNMENT

DE DEFENSIVE END
DE DEFENSIVE TACKLE
LB LINEBACKERS
CB CORNERBACK
S SAFETY

22

LB   **LB**

DE   **DT**

TE **T** **G** **C**

QB

OFFENSIVE TEAM

C CENTER
G GUARD
T TACKLE
TE TIGHT END
WR WIDE RECEIVER
QB QUARTERBACK
RB RUNNING BACK

RB

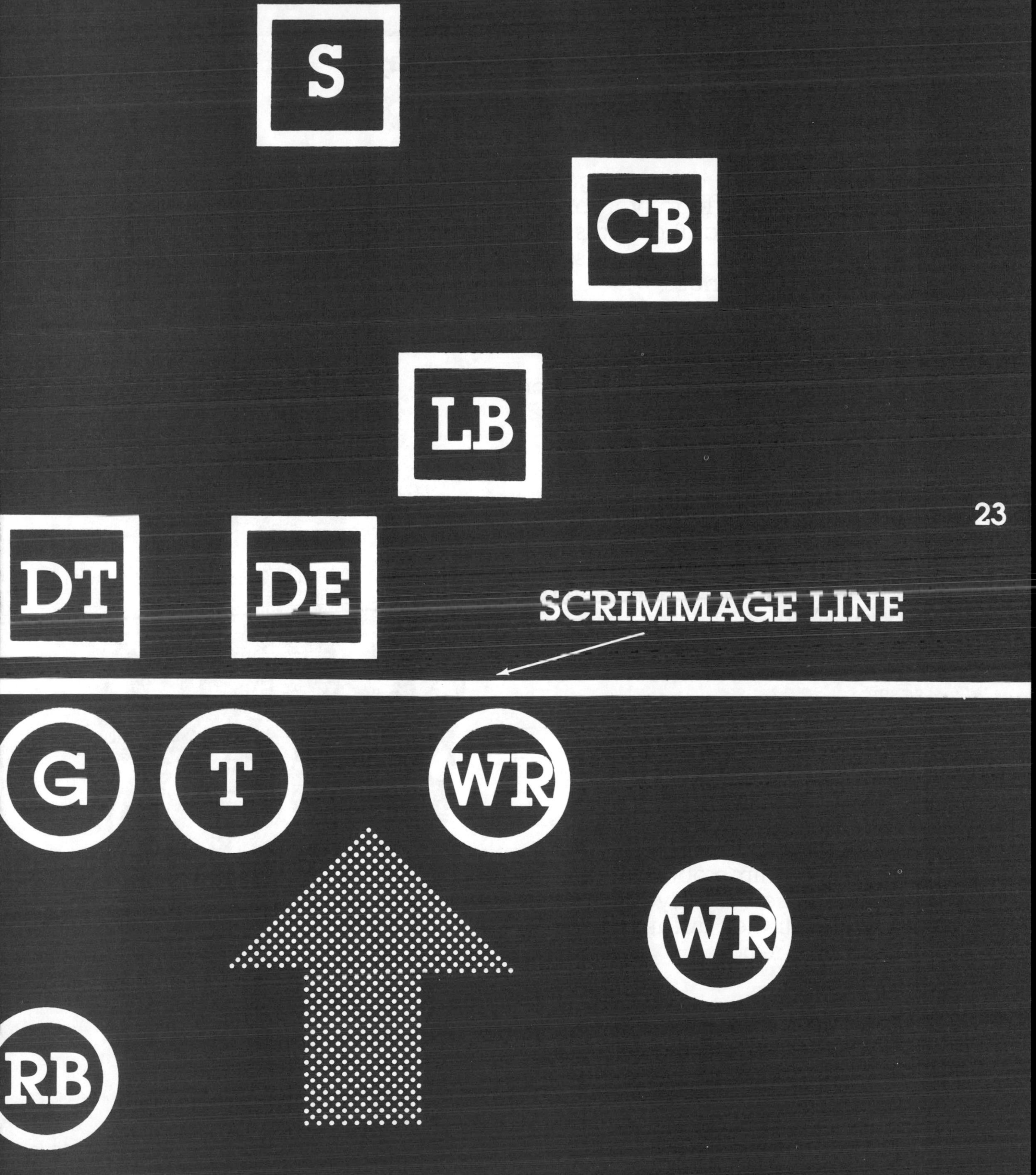

S

CB

LB

23

DT DE

SCRIMMAGE LINE

G T WR

WR

RB

9
TIME-OUTS

Time-outs occur during a game when play is not legally in progress and the official clock is stopped. Automatic time-outs occur in these instances:

- following a touchdown or field goal
- during a try-for-point attempt
- when the ball goes out-of-bounds
- when a receiver makes a fair catch
- at the end of a down when a foul occurs
- when the line judge signals there are two minutes remaining to play in the half
- at the end of a period
- following a change in possession
- when a kicked ball is illegally touched

In addition, each team is allowed three 1 1/2 minute time-outs each half. The referee can also allow a time-out of 2 minutes duration when a player is injured, and of 3 minutes duration for equipment repair.

24

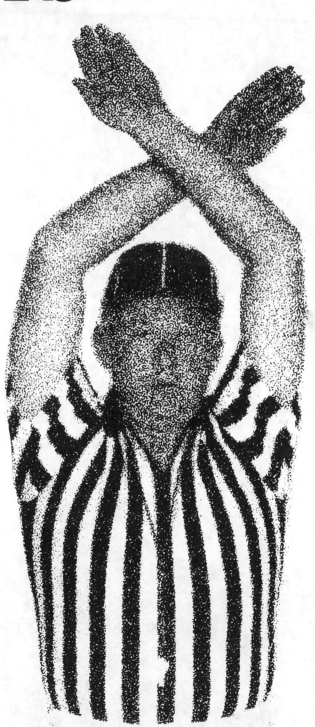

OFFICIAL'S SIGNAL **TIME-OUT**

NO TIME-OUT OR TIME-IN WITH WHISTLE

10
SUBSTITUTION

Substitutes may enter the field only when the ball is dead (not in play). Players must leave on their own side of the field between the endlines, and must do so before the ensuing snap.

11

STARTING PLAY

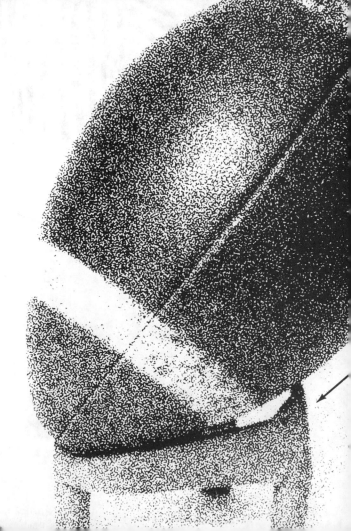

Within 3 minutes of the kick-off, the captains of the opposing teams meet at the center of the field for the coin toss. The visiting team captain calls the toss. The winner of the toss can choose either to receive or kick, or pick the goal his team will defend. The loser of the toss gets the alternative choice. At the beginning of the second half, the captain of the team that lost the toss chooses between the two options.

At the beginning of each half, after a field goal, and after a try for extra point, play is started with a kick-off from the 35-yard line between the inbound lines. After a safety, play is started with a free kick from the 20-yard line.

KICKING OFF

The kick-off may be taken from a tee, another player may hold the ball for the kicker, or the ball can be drop kicked. In the case of a free kick after a safety, the ball can be punted.

At the time of the kick-off, all players must be behind the ball. Players of the opposition team must be at least 10 yards away.

To become in play, the ball must travel at least 10 yards or be touched by a member of the receiving team. Then, the ball must be rekicked if it goes out-of-bounds. The kicking team is penalized 5 yards in such cases.

Once the opposing team gains possession of the ball after a kick-off, or following a free kick after a safety, the team may advance the ball.

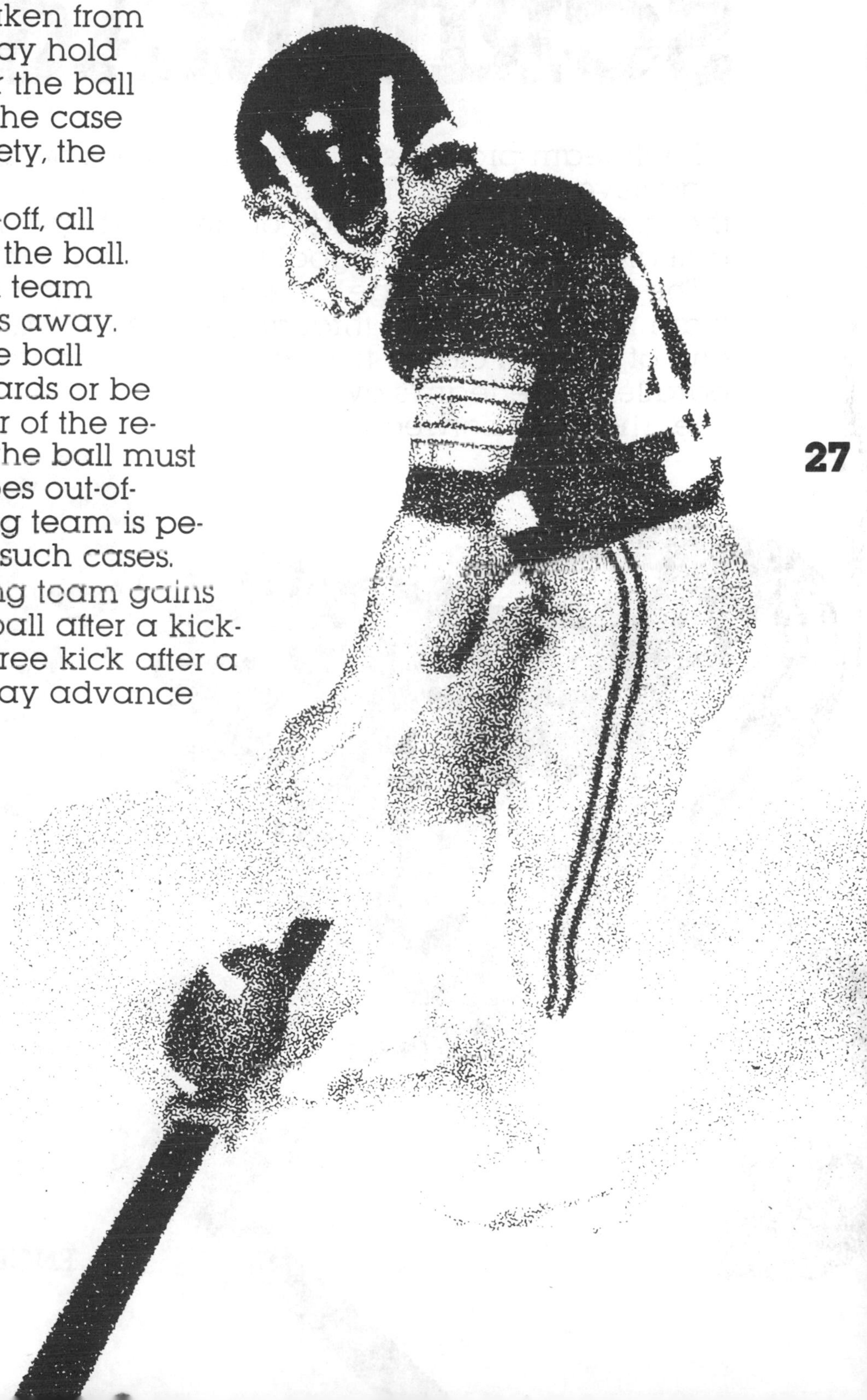

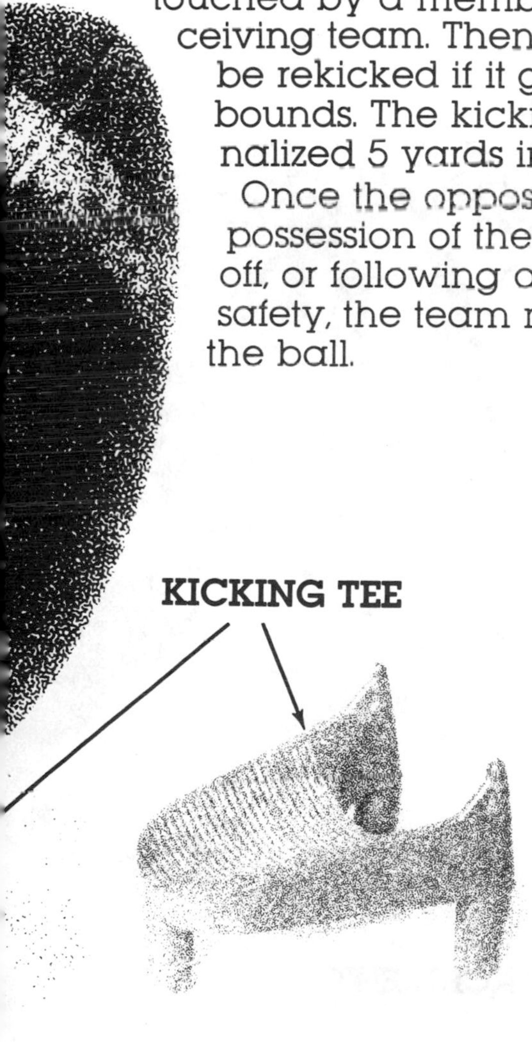

27

KICKING TEE

13

LINE OF SCRIMMAGE

Each team provides a line of at least seven players. They take their positions on either side of the ball and parallel to the goal line.

The line of scrimmage for each team is a line passing through the end of the ball closest to and parallel to the team's own goal line. The area between the two lines of scrimmages is the neutral zone.

The remaining players on each team, except for the player who is to receive the snap, must be at least 1 yard behind the line of scrimmage.

28

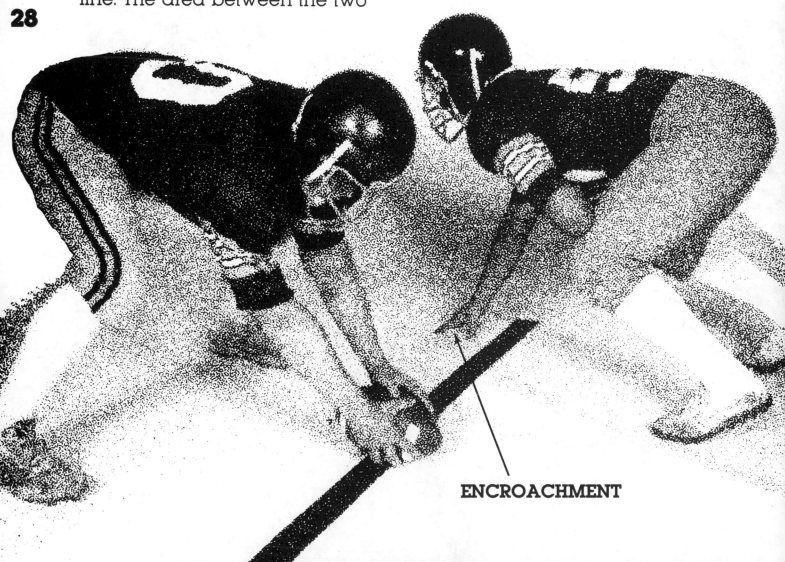

ENCROACHMENT

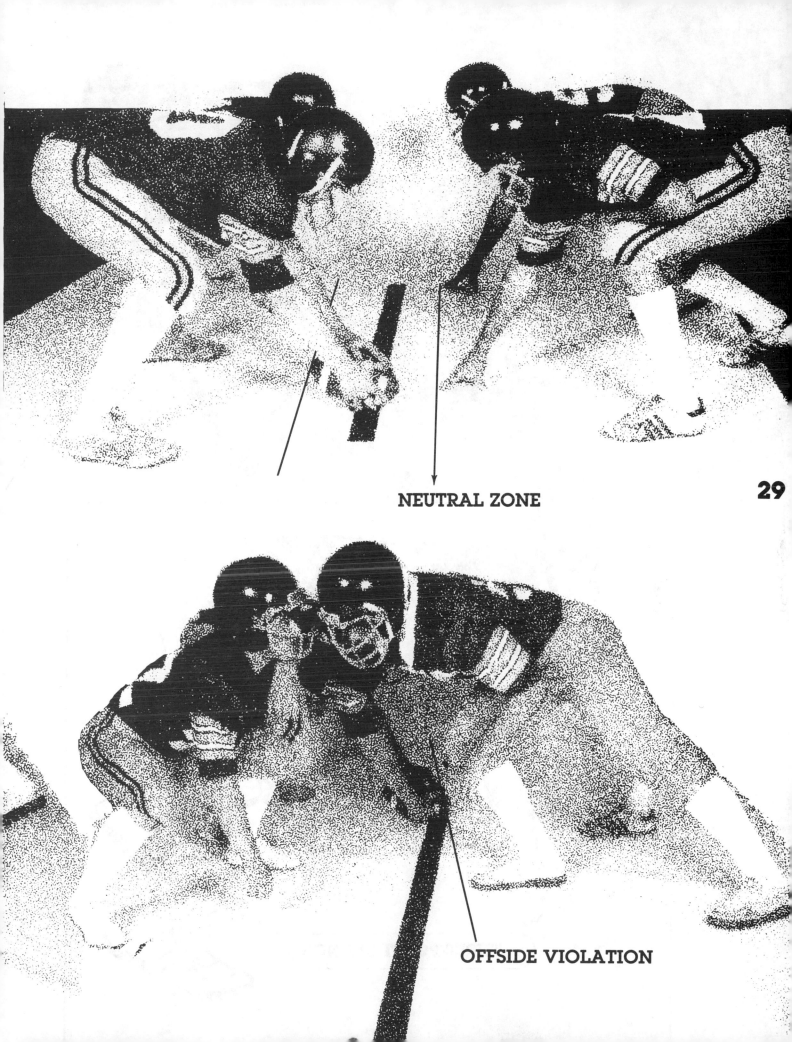

NEUTRAL ZONE

OFFSIDE VIOLATION

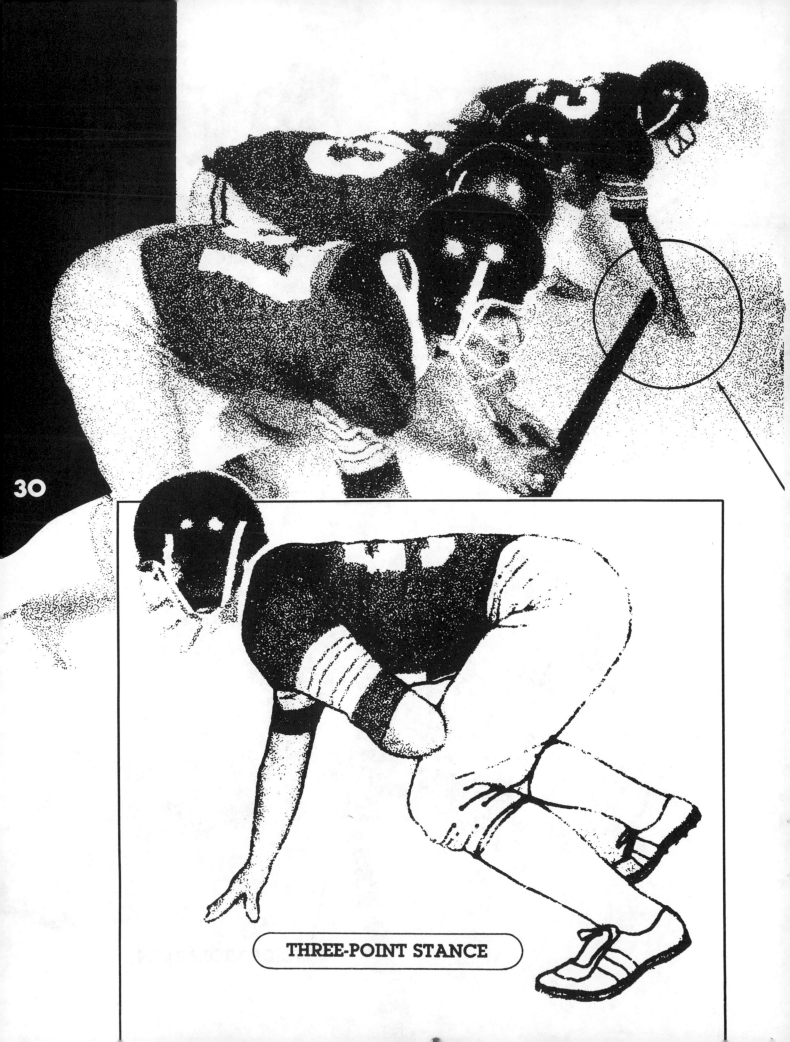

THREE-POINT STANCE

Football Rules

OFFICIAL'S SIGNAL

OFFSIDE OR ENCROACHMENT

14

THE SNAP

The snap is a backward pass directed through the legs of one of the players in the line which puts the ball in play. It must be one quick and continuous action. The snapper is not permitted to slide his hands along the ball before grasping it, nor can he move his feet or lift his hands until after the snap. Other players must remain stationary until the ball is snapped.

Football Rules

33

15

PLAYING THE BALL

A team in possession of the ball is allowed 30 seconds to put the ball in play. A down is the period of action starting from the moment the ball is put in play and that ends when the ball becomes dead.

OFFICIAL'S SIGNAL

DELAY OF GAME OR EXCESS TIME-OUT

MOVING WITH THE BALL

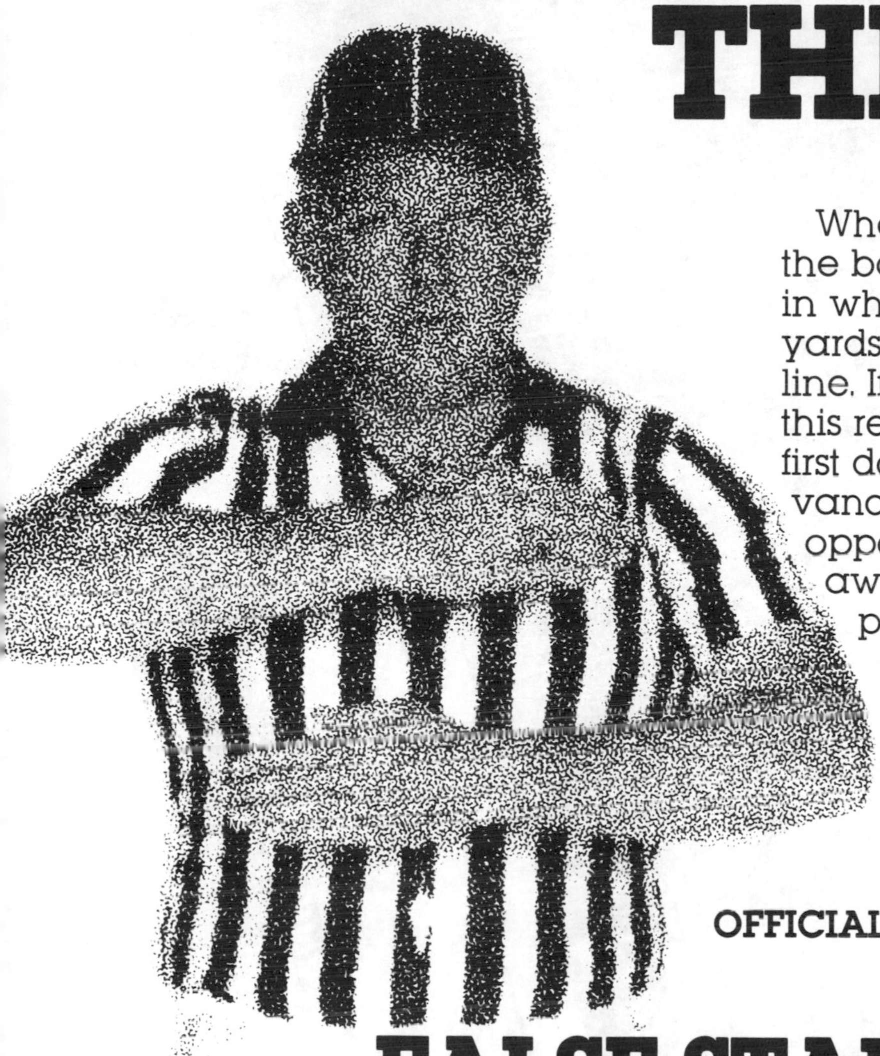

When a team has possession of the ball, it is allowed four downs in which to advance the ball 10 yards or to the opponents' goal line. If the team is successful in this regard, it is permitted another first down. If the team fails to advance the ball 10 yards or to the opponent's goal line, the ball is awarded to the opposition at the point where it became dead.

35

Football Rules

OFFICIAL'S SIGNAL

FALSE START, ILLEGAL SHIFT, ILLEGAL PROCEDURE, ILLEGAL FORMATION, OR KICK-OFF OR SAFETY KICK OUT-OF-BOUNDS

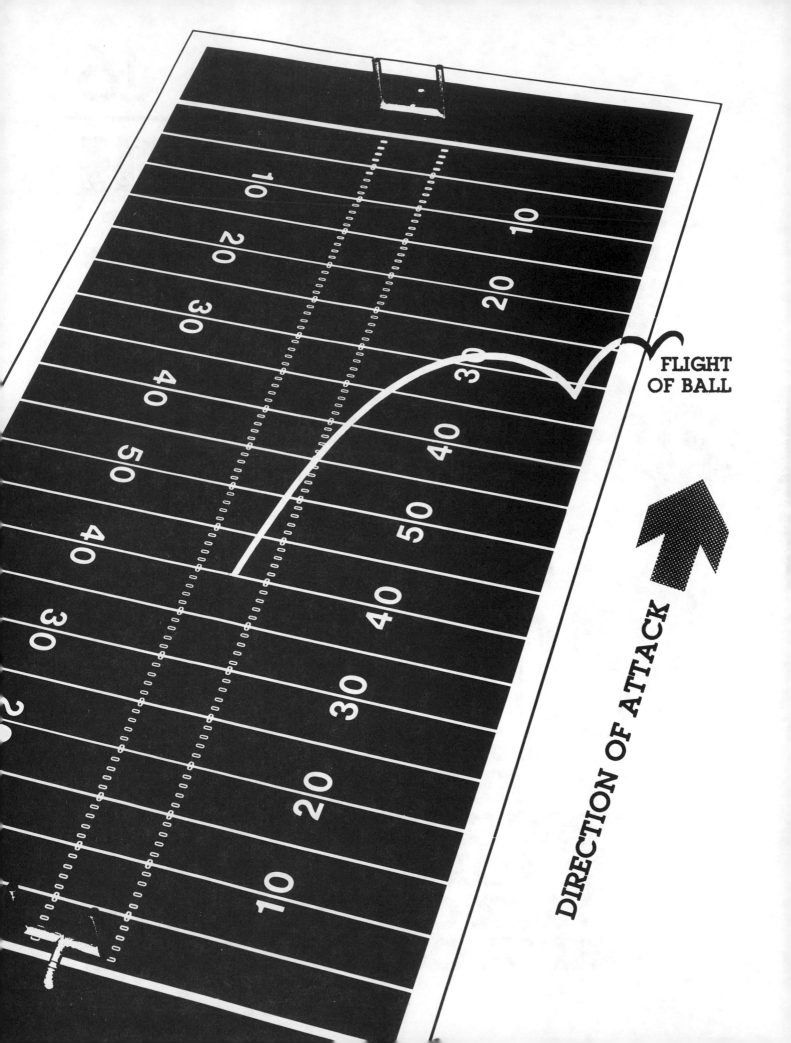

FLIGHT OF BALL

DIRECTION OF ATTACK

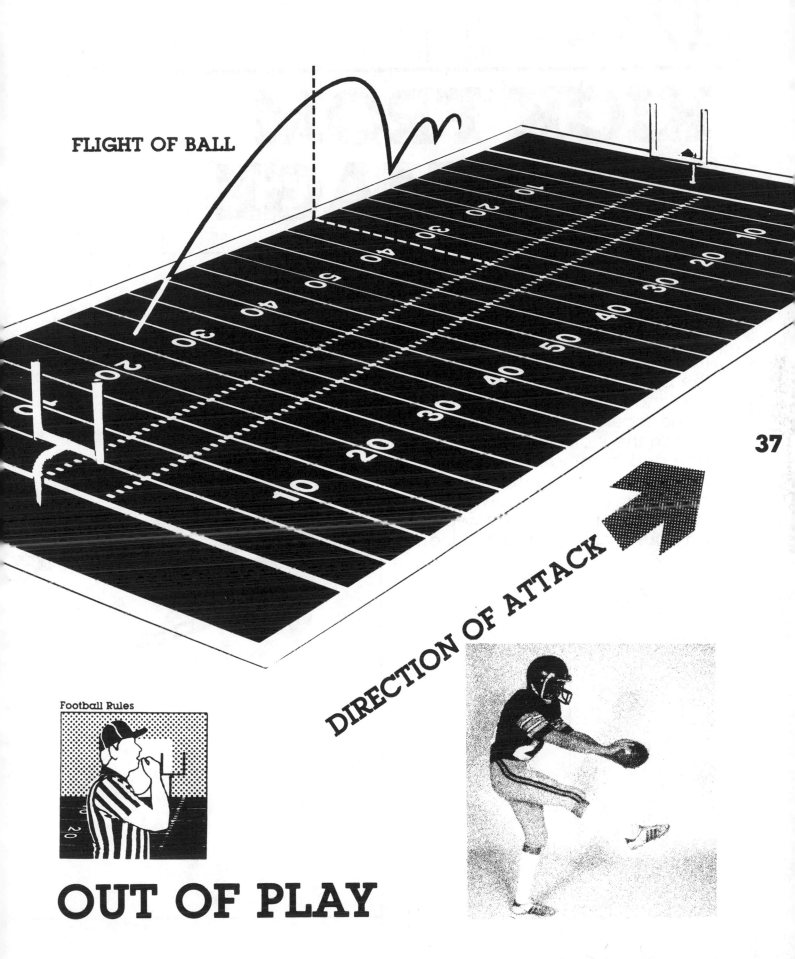

FLIGHT OF BALL

DIRECTION OF ATTACK

37

Football Rules

OUT OF PLAY

17
KICK FROM SCRIMMAGE

A kick from scrimmage, meant to surrender the ball downfield, is called a punt. It involves kicking the ball with the instep before it touches the ground. The team that does the kicking can recover the ball, but is not permitted to advance it.

The receiving team can advance the kick by catching the ball and running upfield with it. If a player receiving the ball fumbles the catch, or merely touches the ball, it can be recovered by any other player on either team.

Football Rules

PUNT

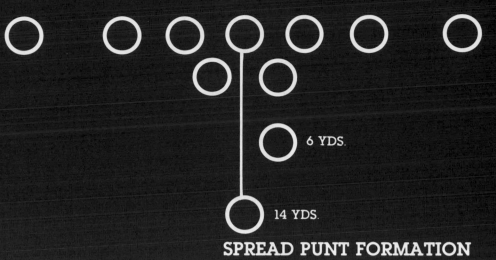

6 YDS.

14 YDS.

SPREAD PUNT FORMATION

Football Rules

RUNNING INTO THE KICKER

39

40

OFFICIAL'S SIGNAL

PERSONAL FOUL

DEAD BALL OR NEUTRAL ZONE ESTABLISHED

OFFICIAL'S SIGNAL

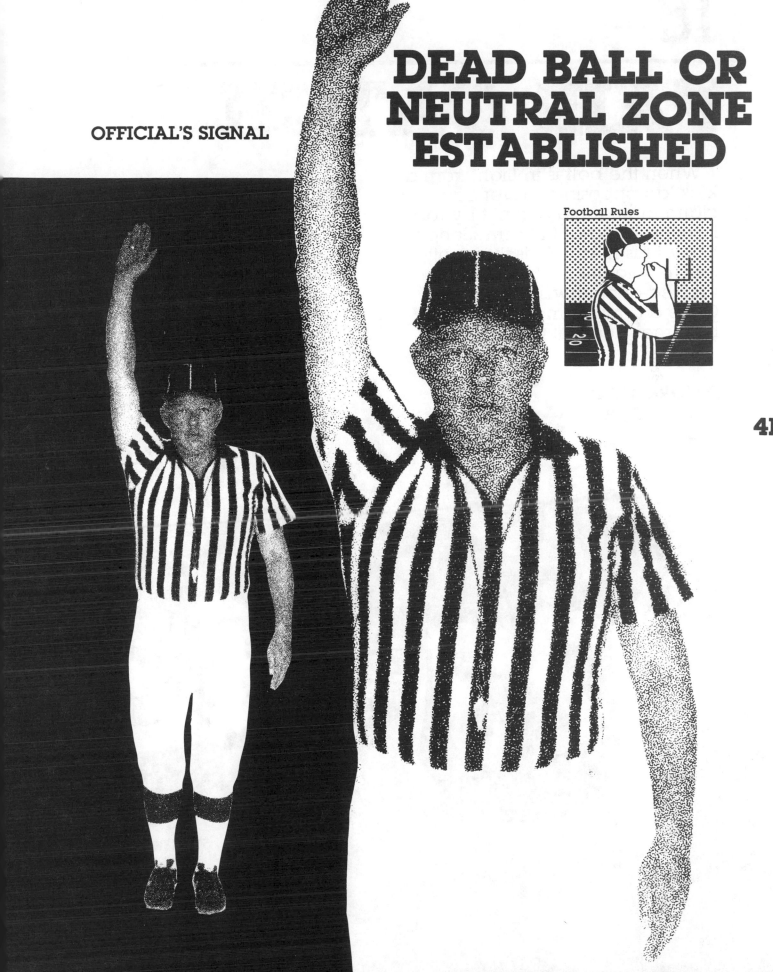

Football Rules

41

18
FAIR CATCH

When the ball is in flight from a kick, an opposing player can claim the right to catch it by raising one hand at full arm's length above his head. He is then entitled to field the ball without being tackled or otherwise impeded. Once a catch is made, the ball becomes dead at that spot.

SIGNAL FOR FAIR CATCH

MAXIMUM OF TWO STEPS AFTER FAIR CATCH

INCORRECT SIGNAL FOR FAIR CATCH

Football Rules

43

OFFICIAL'S SIGNAL

INVALID FAIR CATCH SIGNAL

19 FORWARD PASS

The team in possession of the ball is permitted one forward pass during each play from scrimmage. In order for the pass to be legal, the passer must be behind his line of scrimmage when the ball is thrown. Any other forward pass by either team is illegal.

On the passer's team, only ends or backfield players are permitted to receive the ball. All opposing players are eligible receivers. If an opposing player touches the ball, all players on the passer's team are then eligible to receive the ball.

On any forward pass, the ball becomes dead if it:
- goes out of play
- hits the ground
- hits a goal post or crossbar.

Football Rules

OFFICIAL'S SIGNAL

45

ILLEGAL FORWARD PASS

Football Rules

OFFICIAL'S SIGNAL

INTENTIONAL GROUNDING OF PASS

**PASS
INTERFERENCE**

47

OFFICIAL'S SIGNAL

INTERFERENCE WITH FORWARD PASS OR FAIR CATCH

RECEIVER AND DEFENSIVE BACK VIE FOR PASS

Football Rules

48

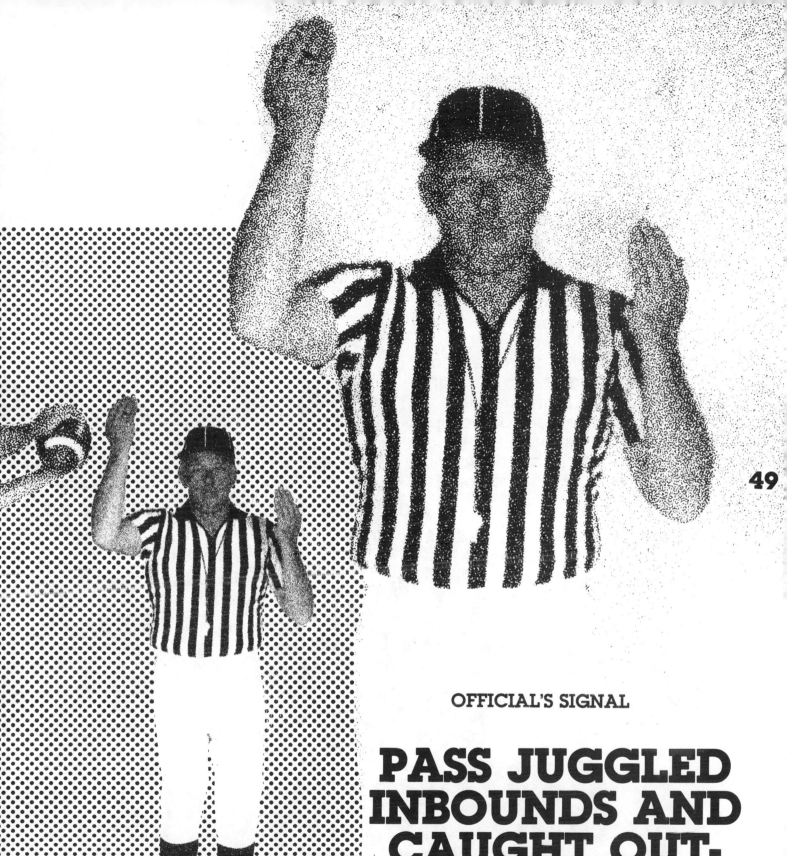

49

OFFICIAL'S SIGNAL

PASS JUGGLED INBOUNDS AND CAUGHT OUT-OF-BOUNDS

20
BACKWARD PASS

A runner may pass the ball backward or laterally at any time. Any player on either team is permitted to catch the pass or to recover it should it touch the ground. If a member of the opposing team recovers the ball after it has touched the ground, the ball is dead and cannot be advanced.

Football Rules

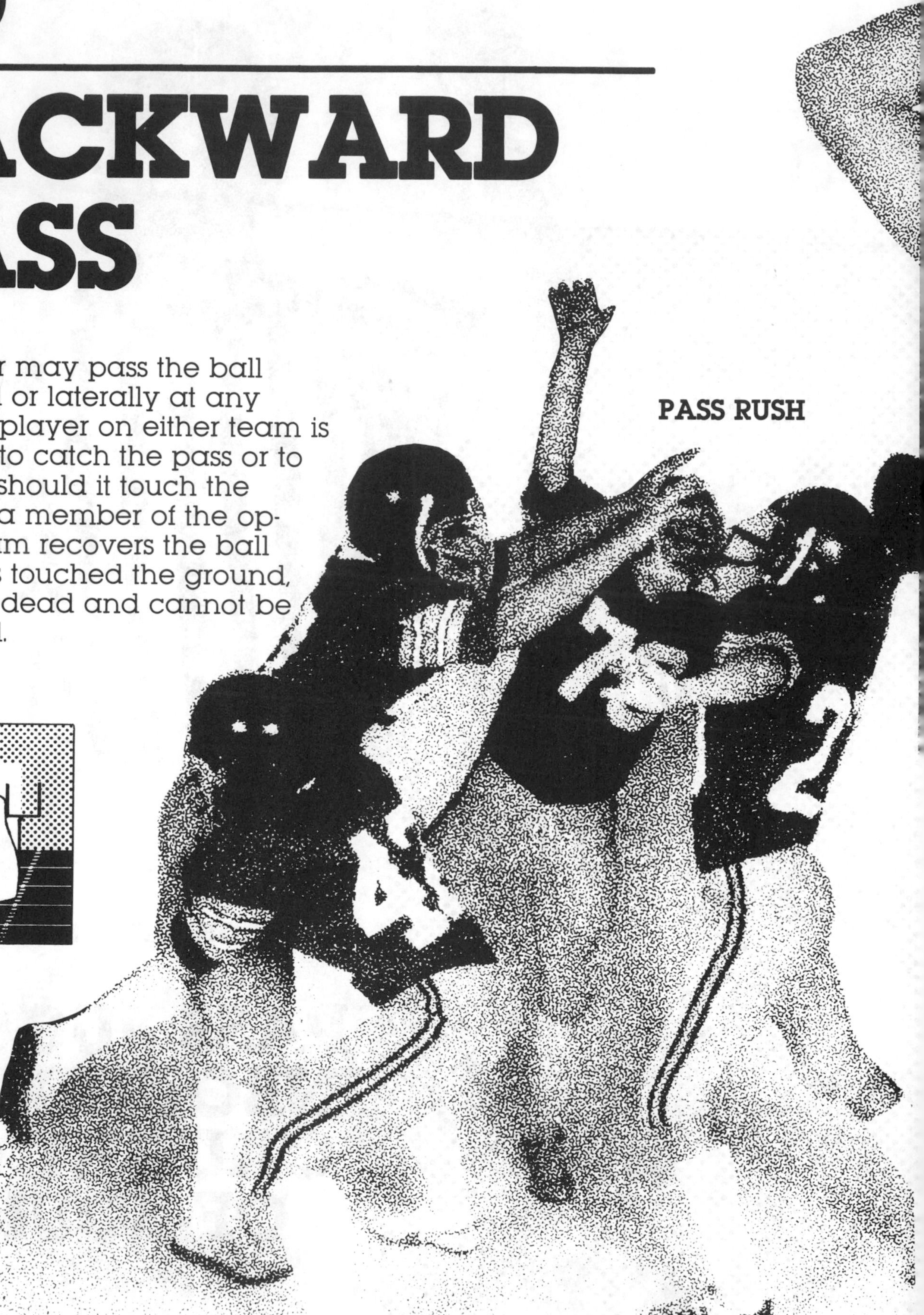

PASS RUSH

Football Rules

OFFICIAL'S SIGNAL

INELIGIBLE RECEIVER OR INELIGIBLE MEMBER OF KICKING TEAM DOWNFIELD

OFFICIAL'S SIGNAL

FIRST DOWN

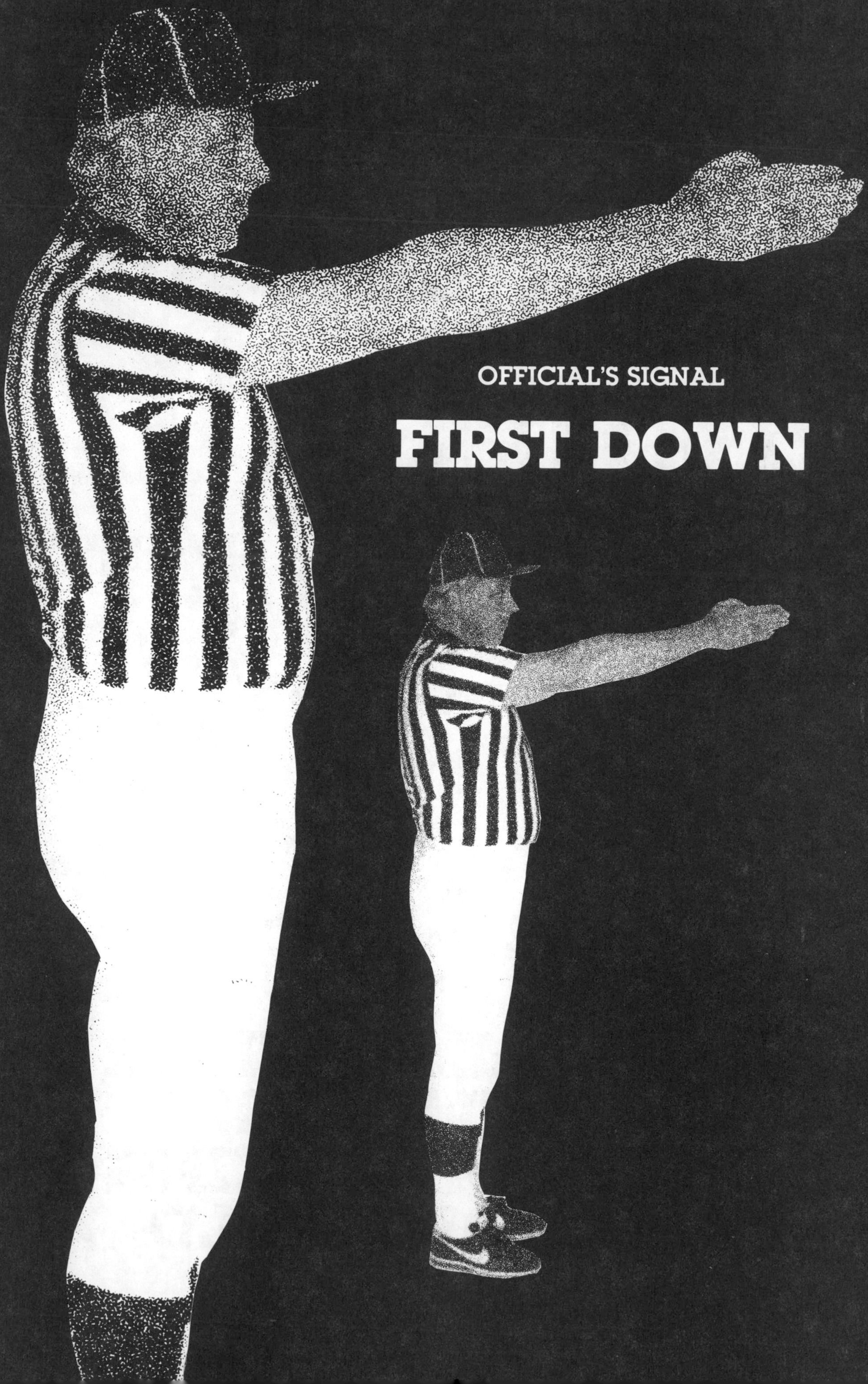

LOSS OF DOWN

21
FUMBLE

If a runner fumbles the ball, play continues, no matter which team makes the recovery, and whether or not the ball strikes the ground. If the ball is unintentionally fumbled forward, it is regarded as an illegal forward pass.

FUMBLE

55

FUMBLE RECOVERY

22
BLOCKING

Blocking is the use of the body above the knees to obstruct an opponent. In executing a block, the hands must be cupped or closed and positioned on a plane inside the elbows. The blocker is not permitted to lock his hands together or strike a blow with his hands. Any type of pushing or punching is illegal. It is also a foul for the blocker to swing or throw an elbow in a menacing manner.

One player may block an opponent at anytime, provided the blocking attempt does not interfere with a pass reception, a fair catch, a kicker, or a passer.

Football Rules

Football Rules

HOLDING

OFFICIAL'S SIGNAL

ILLEGAL CUT OR BLOCKING BELOW THE WAIST

58

23

ILLEGAL TACTICS

SPEARING

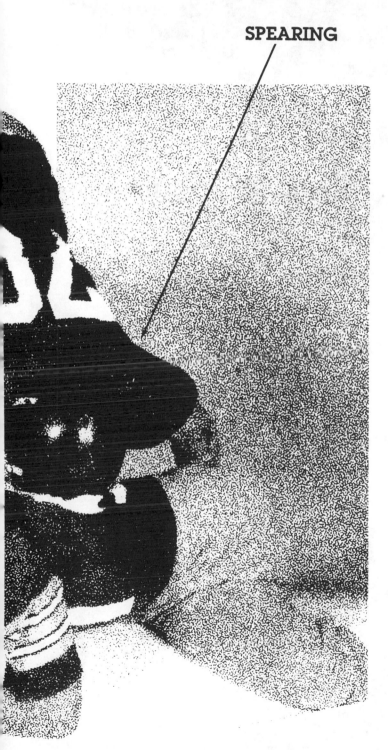

An offensive player is permitted to assist the runner by blocking for him, but the blocker may not:

- push or lift the runner
- cause a teammate to obstruct an opponent
- grasp or tackle an opponent with his hands or arms.

Neither offensive or defensive players are permitted to:

- kick or knee an opponent
- strike an opponent's face, head, or neck with the side, back, or heel of the wrist, or with the forearm or elbow
- trip an opponent
- tackle a player who is off the field
- fall on a downed runner or a runner after the ball is dead
- grasp an opponent's face mask.

Driving one's helmet into an opponent—spearing—is illegal, as is butt blocking, the technique of using the face mask or front part of the helmet in initiating a block.

Overall, any player who acts in an unsportsmanlike manner is to be penalized.

59

Football Rules

CLIPPING

60

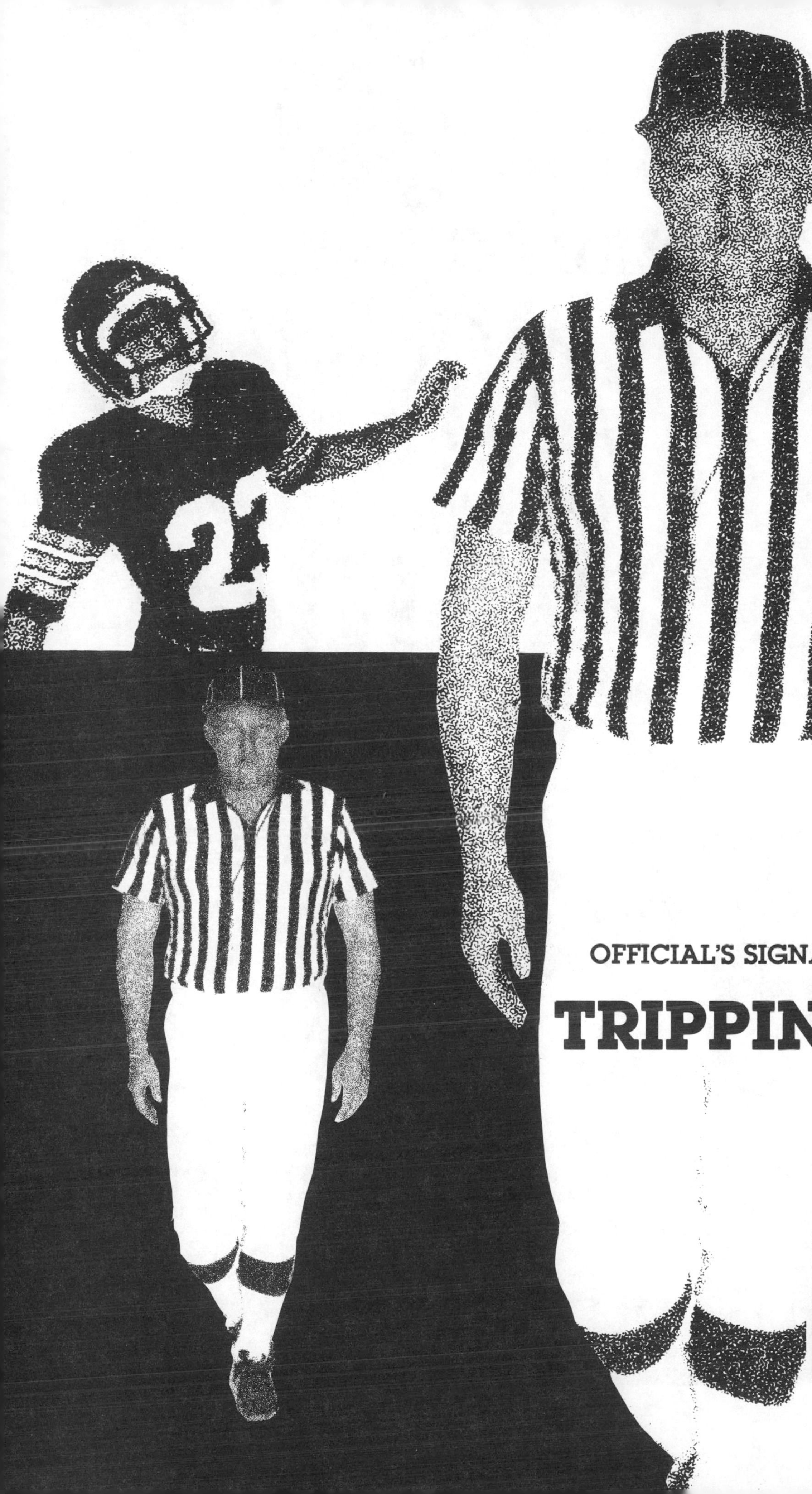

61

OFFICIAL'S SIGNAL

TRIPPING

Football Rules

Football Rules

OFFICIAL'S SIGNAL

HOLDING

62

HOLDING

Football Rules

63

OFFICIAL'S SIGNAL

PENALTY REFUSED, INCOMPLETE PASS, PLAY OVER, OR MISSED GOAL

TWO-POINT STANCE

Football Rules

ROUGHING THE PASSER

64

ILLEGAL CRACKBACK

65

Football Rules

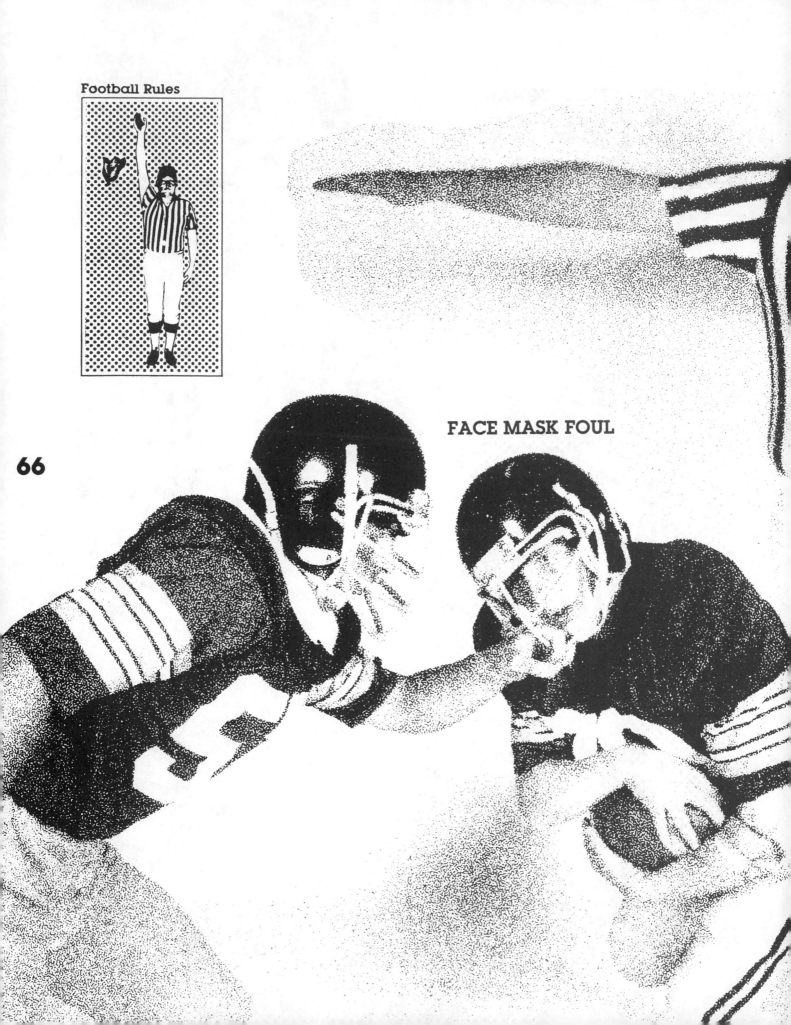

Football Rules

66

FACE MASK FOUL

UNSPORTSMANLIKE CONDUCT
(Non-contact fouls)

67

Football Rules

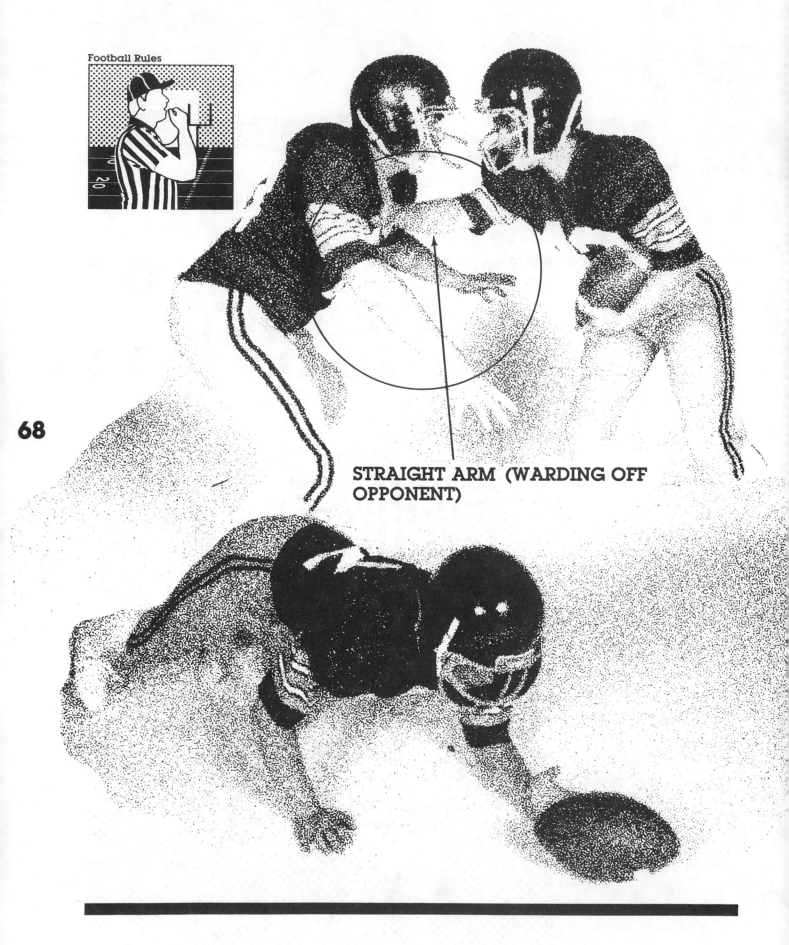

Football Rules

68

STRAIGHT ARM (WARDING OFF OPPONENT)

OFFICIAL'S SIGNAL

CRAWLING, INTERLOCKING INTERFERENCE, PUSHING, OR HELPING RUNNER

Football Rules

Football Rules

OFFICIAL'S SIGNAL

BALL ILLEGALLY TOUCHED, KICKED, OR BATTED

TOUCHING A FORWARD PASS OR SCRIMMAGE KICK

OFFICIAL'S SIGNAL

Football Rules

ILLEGAL INTERFERENCE

Contacting the ball, an opposing player, or moving into the path of an opposing player becomes illegal interference in any one of the following situations:

• After a receiver has signaled for a fair catch. No player of the kicking team may touch the ball or interfere with the receiver's attempt to make the catch.

• After a kicker has kicked the ball from behind the line of scrimmage. No defensive player is permitted to charge into the kicker. An exception occurs when the kick has been partially blocked and the defensive player's momentum carries him into the kicker.

• After a passer has passed the ball. No defensive player is permitted to charge into the passer. An exception can occur in cases where the momentum of the defensive player in his attempt to block the pass brings him into contact with the passer.

• During a forward pass. No defensive player is to hinder the progress of an eligible receiver in his attempt to make the catch. An exception can occur when the receiver and defensive player make a simultaneous attempt to catch the same ball.

OFFICIAL'S SIGNAL

ILLEGAL USE OF HANDS

OFFICIAL'S SIGNAL

ILLEGAL MOTION
AT SNAP

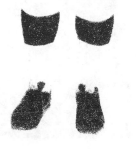

25

FOULS AND PENALTIES

A foul is any violation of a playing rule. When a team is charged with a foul, it loses 5, 10, or 15 yards, depending on the nature of the foul. The various fouls and the penalties for each are listed below:

FOUL	PENALTY
Assisting the runner	Ten yards
Batting or punching loose ball	Fifteen yards
Butting, spearing, or ramming an opponent	Fifteen yards
Clipping	Fifteen yards
Crawling	Five yards
Defensive holding	Five yards plus automatic first down
Delay of game at start of half	Fifteen yards
Encroachment	Five yards
Excessive number of time-outs	Five yards
Failure to pause one second after shift or huddle	Five yards
Fair catch interference	Fifteen yards
False start	Five yards
Forward pass out-of-bounds	Loss of down
Forward pass strikes ground, goal post or goal post crossbar	Loss of down
Forward pass thrown beyond the line of scrimmage	Five yards plus loss of down

FOUL	PENALTY
Forward pass thrown from behind the line of scrimmage after ball once crossed line	Loss of down
Forward pass touches ineligible receiver	Loss of down
Grasping opponent's face mask	Five yards
Illegal blocking below the waist	Fifteen yards
Illegal crackback block	Fifteen yards
Illegal formation	Five yards
Illegal motion	Five yards
Illegal return	Five yards
Illegal shift	Five yards
Illegal substitution	Five yards
Illegal use of hands	Five yards plus automatic first down
Illegal use of hands by offense, holding	Ten yards
Ineligible member of kicking team downfield before ball is kicked	Five yards
Ineligible player downfield on passing down	Ten yards
Intentionally kicking loose ball	Fifteen yards
Invalid fair catch signal	Five yards
Kick-off out-of-bounds	Five yards
Less than 7 players on offensive line at snap	Five yards
More than 11 players on field at snap	Five yards
More than one man in motion at snap	Five yards

FOUL	PENALTY
Offensive pass interference	Ten yards
Offside	Five yards
Piling on	Fifteen yards plus automatic first down
Player out-of-bounds at snap	Five yards
Pulling an opponent by face mask	Fifteen yards
Roughing the kicker	Fifteen yards plus automatic first down
Roughing the passer	Fifteen yards plus automatic first down
Running into kicker	Five yards plus automatic first down
Second forward pass behind the line	Loss of down
Tripping	Ten yards
Unnecessary roughness	Fifteen yards
Unsportsmanlike conduct	Fifteen yards

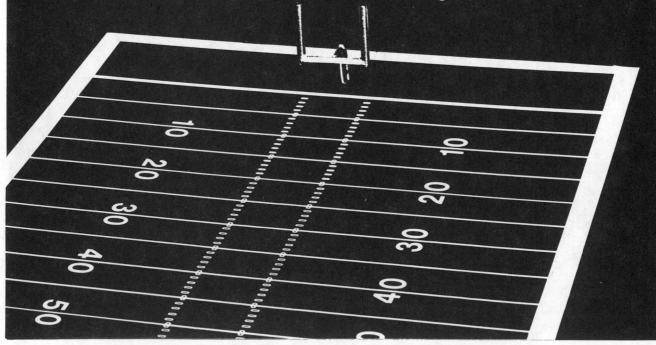

Football Rules

OFFICIAL'S SIGNAL

PLAYER
DISQUALIFIED

26

SCORING

OFFICIAL'S SIGNAL

A touchdown—6 points—occurs when a player carries the ball to the opponent's end zone and touches the goal line with the ball, or recovers a loose ball on or behind the opposition goal line.

After a touchdown, the scoring team is allowed to try for one additional point. The ball is placed down between the inbound lines and at least 2 yards from the goal line. The point may be scored by a run, pass, or place kick. As soon as the defensive team gains possession of the ball, causes a pass to go incomplete, or blocks a kick, the ball is dead.

A field goal—3 points—occurs when a player kicks the whole of the ball through the opponent's goal by means of a place kick or a drop kick, without the ball touching the ground or any of his teammates. After a missed field goal attempt, the ball is returned to the line of scrimmage or the 20-yard line, whichever is farther from the goal line.

A safety occurs when a team sends the ball into its own end zone and it becomes dead in its possession, or out of play behind its own goal line.

78

TOUCHDOWN, FIELD GOAL, OR SUCCESSFUL TRY

OFFICIAL'S SIGNAL
SAFETY

79

PLAYER TACKLED IN OWN END ZONE (SAFETY)

27

GLOSSARY

back A member of the offensive backfield, that is, the quarterback or one of the running backs; also, one of the members of the defensive secondary—either of the two safeties or cornerbacks.

blind-side block A block directed at a player by an unseen opponent.

blitz A surprise defensive maneuver in which one or more linebackers and/or safeties charge across the line of scrimmage in an effort to sack the quarterback.

block To check a defensive player by means of legal body contact. The offensive player is permitted to use any part of his body above his knees. If he uses his arms, however, he must keep them close to his body.

blocked kick Any punt, field goal, or try-for-point attempt that is deflected or stopped by the defensive team.

brush block Quick, light contact on the part of an offensive player to delay a defensive man's charge.

center To snap the ball back from the line of scrimmage.

chain crew The group of three assistants to the officials—a box-man and two rodmen—who handle the first-down yardage equipment.

CENTER

chucking To ward off an opponent who is in front of a defender by contacting him with a quick extension of the arm or arms, followed by the return of arm(s) to a flexed position, thereby breaking the original contact.

clipping To throw the body across the back of an opponent's leg or to hit him from the rear while moving up from behind, unless the opponent is a runner or the action is in close line play.

completion A forward pass legally caught.

conversion The 1-point score made in try-for-point attempt.

crackback block A block delivered by an eligible receiver in which he starts downfield as if running a pattern, then turns back to take out a linebacker or defensive end. The block may not be delivered below the waist.

crawling An attempt to advance the ball after the officials' whistle has sounded.

crossbar The horizontal bar connecting the goalpost uprights.

cut Any quick change of direction on the part of a runner or receiver.

defensive backfield The four-man unit that consists of the two cornerbacks and two safeties.

defensive holding Illegal use of the hands while blocking an offensive player.

defensive line The two tackles and two ends.

CLIPPING

delay of game Any action—or inaction—by either team which prevents the ball from being put in play promptly.

direct pass A pass from the center to a backfield man or other player positioned several yards behind the line of scrimmage, as in the case of the center's pass to the punter.

disqualified player A player who is banished from the game for committing any one of a number of what the rulebook calls "palpably unfair acts," including kneeing or kicking an opponent, striking him with the fists, or flagrant roughing of the passer or kicker.

double foul A rule infraction by both teams on the same down.

down   The period of action that starts when the ball is put in play and ends when it is dead.

drop kick   A type of kick in which the ball is dropped to the ground and kicked just as it rebounds from the ground.

encroachment   Movement by a player, usually a lineman, across the neutral zone before the ball's snap in which he makes contact with an opposing player.

end lines   The lines at each end of the field.

end zones   The areas at each end of the field bounded by the end lines, side lines, and goal lines.

extra point   The one-play, one-point scoring opportunity given a team that scores a touchdown.

fair catch   An unhindered catch of a kick by a member of the receiving team who must raise one arm full length above his head while the kick is in flight.

field goal   Three points, earned when a place kick goes over the crossbar and between the uprights (extended indefinitely upward) of the goal posts.

first down   A team has four downs in which to gain ten yards; a "first down" is earned when it gains a sufficient number of yards to be entitled to another sequence of four downs.

forward pass   A ball thrown toward the opposition goal line.

foul   Any violation of a playing rule.

free kick   A play in which the defensive team is restrained from interfering with the kicker. It can occur as a kick-off, kick after a safety, or kick after a fair catch. It can take the form of a place kick, drop kick, or punt (except a punt cannot be used on a kick-off).

fumble   A ball in play after having been dropped or otherwise mishandled.

goal line   The line that separates the field of play from the end zone. There are goal lines 10 yards from and parallel to each of the end lines.

goalpost   Either of the two upright poles at each end of the field. The goalposts are 18 1/2 feet apart and connected by a cross-bar that is 10 feet above the ground.

halftime The 15-minute intermission between halves of a game.

handoff The exchange of the ball from one offensive player to another.

illegal procedure Movement on the part of a member of the offensive line after the team is set and before the ball is snapped.

impetus The action of a player which gives momentum to the ball.

in-bounds lines The two series of short lines that run the length of the field. Each is 70 feet, 9 inches from the near side line.

incompletion A forward pass that is not completed.

ineligible receiver An offensive player, normally an interior tackle, guard, or center, not permitted to catch a forward pass.

intentional grounding An infraction of the rules in which a passer deliberately throws an incomplete pass in order to avoid being tackled behind the line of scrimmage.

interception A pass caught by a defensive player.

interference The offensive players who block in front of the ball carrier.

kick-off A place kick used to begin play at the start of a half or after a score.

lateral A pass that travels to either side or backward.

lineman One of the seven offensive players positioned at the line of scrimmage—the center, two guards, two tackles, and two ends.

line of scrimmage The imaginary line from side line to side line through the ball that separates the offense and defense at the beginning of each play.

live ball A ball legally free-kicked or snapped.

loose ball A ball in play not in possession of any player.

muff For a player to touch a loose ball in an unsuccessful attempt to gain possession.

multiple foul Two or more fouls by the same team on the same down.

neutral zone The area between the offensive and defensive lines of scrimmage. It is the length of the ball in width.

offense The team in possession of the ball.

offensive holding Illegal use of the hands while blocking a defensive player.

official Any one of the members of the seven-man officiating team charged with the responsibility of regulating play and enforcing the rules.

off-setting penalties A situation that occurs when both teams are guilty of rule infractions on the same down. The penalties cancel out each other.

offside The situation that occurs when any part of a player's body is beyond his scrimmage line or free kick line when the ball is snapped.

onside kick A short kick-off by means of which the kicking team hopes to gain possession of the ball. (Actually, all kick-offs are onside kicks, since the term "onside" refers to the area of the field to which the play is directed.)

pass interference Illegal interference with a player's opportunity to catch a forward pass or make an interception.

penalty A punishment, handicap, or loss of advantage imposed upon a team for a rule infraction.

penalty marker The handkerchief-size yellow flag carried by an official and thrown to the ground to indicate a rule violation.

personal foul　An instance of il-legal hitting, such as unnecessary roughness, clipping, piling on, kicking, punching, or running into the passer or kicker.

piling on　Falling upon or throwing oneself upon a downed ball carrier after the whistle has sounded.

place kick　A kick executed while the ball is in a fixed position on the ground, either on a tee or held by a teammate.

placement　A place kick.

pocket　The protected area formed by the five interior line-men in which the quarterback sets up to throw.

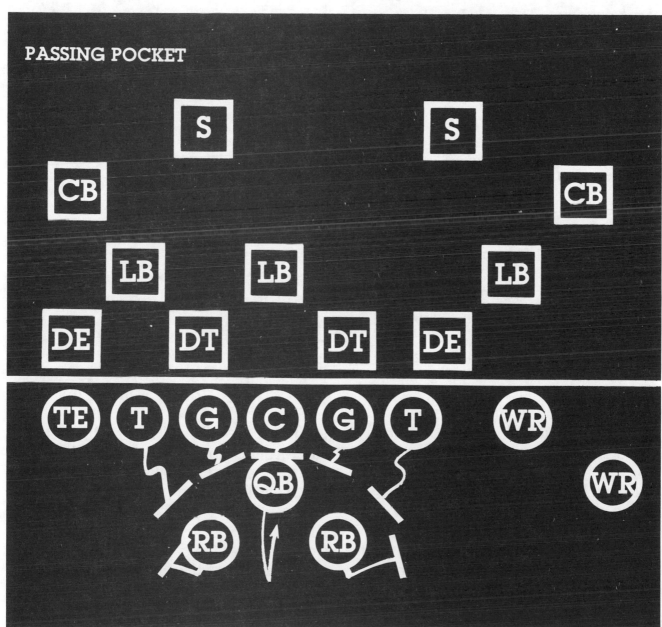

PASSING POCKET

possession A rulebook term that refers to any player who holds and controls the ball long enough "to perform any act common to the game."

punt A kick from scrimmage made when a player drops the ball and kicks it while it is in flight.

punt return The runback of a punt.

quarter One of the four 15-minute periods that constitute a game; a period.

recover To gain possession of a fumbled ball.

return A runback of a kick, punt, or an intercepted pass.

roughing the kicker To run into the kicker in a violent manner.

rushing Running with the ball on a play from scrimmage.

sack To tackle or otherwise dump the quarterback for a loss while he is attempting to pass.

safety A situation in which the ball is dead on or behind a team's own goal, with the impetus coming from a player on that team. Two points are awarded the opposing team.

shift The movement of two or more offensive players at the same time before the snap.

side lines The lines at each side of the field extending from end line to end line.

snap The passing of the football from the center to the quarterback.

spearing An attempt by one player to hurt or injure another by lunging at him helmet first.

sudden death The continuation of a tied game into overtime. The team scoring first (by safety, field goal, or touchdown) wins.

time-out An interval during the game when play is not legally in progress and the official clock is stopped.

touchback A situation that occurs when a ball is dead on or behind a team's own goal line, with the impetus coming from an opponent, provided it is not a touchdown or a missed field goal.

try-for-point The opportunity given a team that has scored a touchdown to add another point by successfully executing a single play from scrimmage. The ball is put in play from the 2-yard line or any point beyond it.

turnover Losing the ball by a fumble or interception.

two-minute warning Official's verbal notification to the head coach that two minutes of playing time remain in the half.

two-point option In college football, a team scoring a touchdown has the option of trying for either one or two points. The ball is placed on the two-yard line. A team is awarded 1 point for a successful place kick, or 2 points for successfully running or passing the ball across the goal line.

unsportsmanlike conduct Any act contrary to the generally understood principles of sportsmanship.

yardage Distance lost or gained by the offensive team on a play from scrimmage.

yard line Any of the lines marked at 5-yard intervals across the field of play between the two goal lines.

CHRONOLOGY OF FOOTBALL RULE CHANGES

1869 Princeton and Rutgers played first college football game at New Brunswick, New Jersey, on successive Saturdays, November 6 and 13. Rutgers won first game, 6-4; Princeton took the second, 8-0.

1876 American Intercollegiate Football Association created at Springfield, Massachusetts. Rules adopted were a modified version of Rugby Union rules.

1877 Teams consisted of 15 players: 9 men on the rush line, 1 quarterback, 2 halfbacks, 1 three-quarter back, and 2 fullbacks. Game 90 minutes in length.

1878 Canvas pants and jackets made mandatory instead of tights and jerseys.

1880 Number of players on side reduced to 11. The rugby "scrum" was replaced by a line of scrimmage. Quarterback was designated as the player to receive the snap from the center. Playing field established at 110 by 53 1/3 yards, replacing field 140 by 70 yards.

1881 Two overtime periods of 15 minutes were established to break ties.

1882 Rules on "downs" and "yards" were introduced, e.g., "If, on 3 consecutive downs, a team has not advanced the ball 5 yards, or lost 10 yards, it must give up the ball to the other side at the spot where the final down is made." Use of signals for calling plays introduced.

THE RUGBY BALL

SPALDING'S LIBRARY OF ATHLETIC SPORTS

TRADE SPALDING MARK

THE
GAME OF FOOT BALL.

PUBLISHED BY

A. G. SPALDING & BROS.

CHICAGO

NEW YORK.

PRICE 10 CENTS.

1883 Reorganization of officials provided for two judges, one to be selected by each team, and one impartial referee, the latter to be the head official.

1884 Scoring system revised, re-establishing these point values:
touchdown: 4 points
goal after touchdown: 2 points
safety: 2 points
goal from field: 5 points

1887 University of Pennsylvania and Rutgers meet in an indoor football game at New York's Madison Square Garden, the first contest of its type.

1888 Rule prohibiting blocking with arms extended introduced; tackling restricted to above the knees.

1894 Length of game reduced from 90 to 70 minutes, divided into halves. Rule adopted forbidding one player from laying hands on opposing player without the ball. Limitation on man-in-motion rule established, mandating that no play can be valid in which three or more men start in motion before the snap.

1897 Scoring system revised, establishing these point values:
touchdown: 5 points
goal after touchdown: 1 point
safety: 2 points
field goal: 5 points

1902 Teams required to change goals following a touchdown or field goal.

1904 Value of field goal reduced to 4 points.

1906 Forward pass introduced. Length of game reduced to 60 minutes. Distance to gain to achieve first down increased to 10 yards. Officials to consist of referee, 2 umpires, and linesman.

1907 One of 2 umpires eliminated in favor of field judge.

1908 First numbering of players, at Washington and Jefferson.

1909 Value of field goal reduced to 3 points.

1910 Substitution rule modified to permit player removed from game to return in subsequent period. Game divided into four 15-minute quarters. Time-out interval between first and second, and third and fourth quarters fixed at one minute, with 30-minute interval established between halves.

1912 Teams given four downs to gain 10 yards and first down. Length of field reduced to 100 yards. An extra space of 10 yards

established behind each goal as an area in which an offensive player could legally catch a forward pass. Point of kick-off, previously executed from mid-field, changed to the 40-yard line of the kicking team. Value of touchdowns increased from 5 to 6 points.

1917 Substitutes prohibited from talking with members of team on the field until completion of first play.

1920 American Professional Football Association, forerunner of the National Football League, formed.

1922 In try-for-point play, ball was to be put in play from the 5-yard line; previously, ball was snapped from spot where ball crossed goal line as touchdown was being scored.

1922 American Professional Football Association changed its name to National Football League.

1924 Players required to come to full stop on plays involving shifts.

1925 Winner of coin toss given choice of receiving kick-off or kicking off to opposing team. Clipping forbidden.

1926 A penalty of 5 yards plus loss of down imposed for any incomplete forward pass after first incomplete pass in series of downs.

92

1927 Time limit of 30 seconds placed on putting ball in play. Limit of 15 seconds placed on huddle. Fumbled punt declared a dead ball.

1929 Two-yard line established as point where try-for-point plays were to be originated.

1930 Rule instituted mandating that backward passes and fumbles going out-of-bounds between goal lines were to be awarded to team last touching ball.

1932 Rules covering high school play published by National Federation of State High School Associations.

1933 Side zone of 10 yards created; thus, when ball became dead, play was resumed 10 yards from side line. Definition of clipping was broadened to include running into the back of any player not in possession of the ball.

1934 NFL legalized forward pass from anywhere behind the line of scrimmage.

1937 Second kick-off following out-of-bounds kick-off disallowed in favor of putting ball in play on receiving team's 20-yard line. Wearing of numbers on jersey front and back made mandatory.

1938 Term "loose ball" adopted to replace "free ball." Intentionally batting or kicking a loose ball to be punished by a 15-yard penalty. Side zone increased to 15 yards.

1940 Time for putting ball into play, including huddle, fixed at 25 seconds.

1941 Free substitution permitted, except during last two minutes of half.

1943 NFL adopted free substitution rule.

1945 Team making second consecutive kick-off out-of-bounds to be penalized by opposition being awarded the ball on its 40-yard line. Three-inch dirt tee permitted for place kicks.

1946 Number of time-outs permitted in half increased from three to four. NFL nullified free substitution rule; substitutions limited to no more than three at one time.

1947 Blocking rule revised so as to require blockers to keep fists against chest. Linemen on offense no longer permitted to pass neutral zone on forward pass until pass is touched.

1948 Use of plastic kicking tee permitted for place kicks.

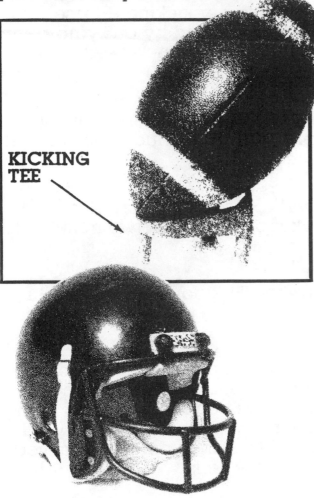

KICKING TEE

1949 NFL adopted free substitution rule. Plastic helmets permitted.

1952 White or brightly colored balls permitted for night-time play.

1955 Sudden death overtime rule tried for first time, on experimental basis, in preseason NFL game between Los Angeles and New York.

1958 In first change in scoring values since 1912, college football mandated that a team scoring a touchdown was to receive the option of trying for 1 or 2 additional points. A successful place kick or drop kick was to be worth 1 point; a successful run or pass, 2 points. All attempts were to be made from the 3-yard line.

1960 American Football League began operation, using 2-point option play following touchdown.

1965 Use of bandages on the forearms and hands to protect injuries made legal. Snapper prohibited from tilting the ball more than 45 degrees.

1966 NFL mandated that goalposts be offset from the goal line, with uprights extending 20 feet above the crossbar. NFL and AFL entered into a merger agreement.

1967 Six-foot wide border around playing field made standard in NFL.

1970 Stadium clock became recognized as official clock.

1971 Determination of intentional grounding made dependent on whether passer was making deliberate attempt to prevent loss of yardage.

1972 In-bounds lines established at 23 yards, 1 foot, 9 inches from side lines, for NFL games.

1974 In NFL, goal posts moved from goal lines to end lines. Kickoffs to be made from 35-yard line, not 40-yard line. After missed field goal, ball to be returned to line of scrimmage or 20-yard line, whichever was farthest from goal line.

1976 Player prohibited from making initial contact with face mask or helmet in blocking or tackling.

1977 In NFL, rule modification made it illegal to strike an opponent above the shoulders during initial charge of defensive lineman. Crackback block also made illegal.

1978 In NFL, rule change permitted defender to maintain contact on receiver within five yards of line of scrimmage, but banned contact beyond that point.

1980 In NFL, players on receiving team prohibited from blocking below the waist on kick-offs, punts, or field goal attempts.

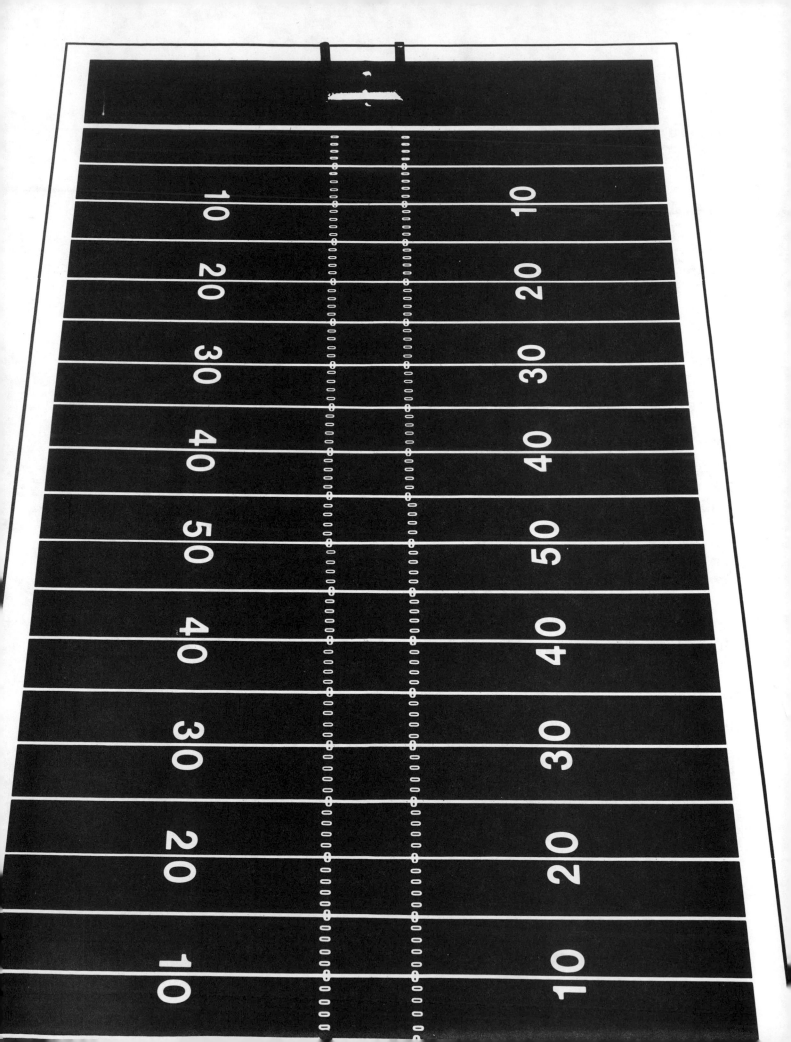